THE
DESSERT
COOKBOOK

Frederick E. Kahn, M.D.
Edited by Betty Carol

Nautilus Communications, Inc.
New York, N.Y.

Published by Nautilus Communications, Inc.
460 East 79th Street, New York, N.Y. 10021

Design by Kathleen Cronin Tinkel

Cover illustration by Marilyn Ackerman

Printed in the United States of America

Contents

Preface

In recent years attention has been focused on the need for each of us to take control of our own future. The concept of self-help means that we should be able to choose how we act in various situations. One of those areas of choice is nutrition—the process or act of nourishing one's self. Furthermore, the changes in the way we feed ourselves have undergone a revolution.

In today's world, we spend time eating and making choices in ways that are very different from our ancestors. Before the use of cooking, people ate raw foods. Eventually, mankind discovered that cooking would change the taste of food. By the Roman times, emphasis was placed on the enjoyment of food as an activity, and as such, more attention was paid to its preparation. As our modes of transportation changed different cultures were introduced to foods from other areas of the world. Food preparation, however, remained laborious because of all the activities necessary to make food edible. Preservatives were primitive, at best, and packaging was not in use.

With the advent of industrialization, many changes occurred. First of all food could be transported rapidly over long distances. Refrigeration, packaging, and chemistry, allowed food to remain for prolonged periods of time on our shelves. Along with these changes, food preparation has also dramatically changed. Instead of using wood, we've moved to gas and electric methods of cooking, as well as using microwaves. Food preparation has speeded up in other areas with the advent of tools and machines to cut and process. Agricultural and technological advances have also added another dimension in producing healthier and more bountiful foodstuffs.

The amount of time we have to spend on ourselves is quite different from what our grandparents had. Because of modern conveniences, along with changes in technology, we have much more leisure time. This allows much more time to follow pursuits other than working. Changes in structure of the family have also made us more isolated and the presence of a nuclear-style family, as well as increasing numbers of adult single individuals have promulgated feelings of loneliness. Food, being one of our earliest contacts with our mothers along with feelings of warmth and wholeness, is a direction that we return to when feeling loneliness. Increasing influence of media has also made us focus much more on different brands of food as well as how and what we are eating. We are aware that we can do something to improve or prolong our lives through exercise and better nutrition.

Social changes have also played an important role in our changing notions of food—and eating. There have been dramatic alterations in the relationship of an individual to those around him or her. Family structure has changed, and where once the large, sprawling family units were the norm, we have now adopted the smaller, tightly-knit "nuclear family" style. There are also many more single adults who make up individual households. In both of these situations we are more likely to experience isolation and feelings of loneliness. Psychologists believe that eating is related to the feeling of warmth and security because of their association during infancy. We often eat when feeling lonely, to replace the lost sensation of wholeness that we experience as babies. When we feel this, we may eat too much or eat improperly.

The choice of what and how much food, where and when to eat, and why we are eating, along with an understanding of nutrition, help us develop the essentials of maintaining good health. Coronary heart disease, obesity, dental caries, iron deficiency anemia, and some types of emotional illnesses, result from a lack of attention to what we eat. You may significantly improve your health and increase your life span by being actively concerned about your nutritional intake.

This book will offer you a compendium that is directed toward healthier nutrition. It offers recipes which are designed to reduce excesses of food stuffs which may lead to poor health. It is not a prescription or formula. I take the attitude that there are many different ways to approach life, and as such, the same is true of our eating habits. Thus, this book presents one of those ways in which you can approach the preparation of food—a healthier way!

What you eat, and how you prepare it, is a decision left to each of you. It is your first step toward a more energetic and healthy life.

Frederick E. Kahn, M.D.

Desserts

Desserts

Those of us who are concerned with cooking and eating nutritiously have come to accept that desserts need not be eliminated from our meals. Before we began our national quest for slimness and the movement towards serving only natural, organically grown foods, dessert was thought of as the crown jewel, the grand finale. We've grown to expect and enjoy it. Many people feel a meal is incomplete without it. Now, with a few simple substitutions of ingredients chosen for their freshness and nutritional quality, as well as a little thoughtful planning, desserts can be a healthy, as well as pleasant way to end a meal. In this volume of the *Preparing Foods the Healthy Way* series you will find easy recipes for a wide array of wonderful desserts which will be nutritious and delight the sweet tooth in almost everyone.

The concern about overuse of sugar is widely known and we offer beneficial alternatives, such as honey, maple syrup or molasses. Whole grains and unbleached white flour should be used wherever possible. Instead of baking soda or baking powder, we've tried to substitute yeast and extra egg whites. Many of the cakes are filled with luscious creams because they contain less sugar and more natural nutrients than traditional icings and frostings.

With hearty dinners, for which you'll find recipes in other volumes of this series, the light touch is called for. Try fruity desserts. Less substantial meals demand something with more protein, such as puddings or a cheesecake. In both cases, desserts are one part of the meal which can be made entirely in advance. And what can be more satisfying than baking your own cakes or cookies, even if they're lopsided or irregular—as long as you did it? You can take extra pride in knowing your desserts include many natural ingredients to make them palatable, rather than just providing empty calories.

In the end, however, not every recipe in this book can be said to contribute to good health. There are those that we thought just too special and good to leave out—and for this reason they become even more of a treat.

The real key, however, to proper nutrition—even with desserts—is to eat with an eye towards a balanced diet. Although most people enjoy desserts and sweet foods, the amount you eat will make a difference. Too much of anything is not healthy, and we recommend that you eat sparingly of rich foods. As a result you will enjoy your desserts even more, and be assured of maintaining a balance in your daily diet.

WEIGHTS AND MEASURES

dash — slightly less than ¼ teaspoon
3 teaspoons — 1 tablespoon
2 tablespoons — ⅛ cup — 1 ounce
4 tablespoons — ¼ cup — 2 ounces
5⅓ tablespoons — ⅓ cup
8 tablespoons — ½ cup — 4 ounces
10⅔ tablespoons — ⅔ cup
2 cups — 1 pint — ½ quart — 1 pound
4 cups — 2 pints — 1 quart
4 quarts — 1 gallon
8 dry quarts — 1 peck
4 pecks — 1 bushel

CAN SIZES

8 ounces — 1 cup
12 ounces — 1½ cup
1 pound or 16 ounces — 2 cups
20 ounces — 2½ cups

ABBREVIATIONS

c. – cup(s)
env. – envelope(s)
F. – Fahrenheit
gal. – gallon(s)
in. – inch(es)
med. – medium
min. – minute(s)
oz. – ounce(s)
pkg. – package(s)
pt. – pint(s)
lb. – pound(s)
qt. – quart(s)
sec. – second(s)
T. – tablespoon(s)
t. – teaspoon(s)

Pies and tarts

Pies and tarts

Americans feel the pie is uniquely theirs, hence, the expression "as American as apple pie." The first mention of pies, however, in literature was in 1304 and was spoken of often in the writings of Chaucer and Dickens. The first pies were made with meat or fish and the first fruit pies (notably, apple) appeared before 1600. These fruit pies were open-faced and called tarts in Northern England, Scotland and Ireland. We hope you will enjoy baking these historic treats as they are delicious and easy to make if you follow these hints.

Crusts

Mixing ingredients. Ingredients should always be at room temperature (about 70° F.) before mixing. Many experts use pastry flour which is finer than all-purpose flour but less fine than cake flour for an extra flaky and tender crust. However, you can use all-purpose flour with equally satisfying results. Egg yolks add richness and color to the crust. Measure ingredients carefully as too much flour will cause toughness, too much water will result in sogginess and too much shortening will turn crust crumbly and greasy.

For a perfect crust, handle dough lightly and sparingly. This will incorporate more air and inhibit the development of gluten. Always use lard or shortening, as called for—this produces a much more tender product.

Cutting. For cutting the fat into the flour, use a pastry cutter or two knives, scissoring to the texture of course meal, or finer to create the flakiest crust. Combining the fat and flour with your fingers tends to soften the fat and overblend it, making crust less flaky. Using ice water will promote flakiness. Sprinkle ice water a tablespoon at a time over dough, blending with a fork just until dough forms a ball. The water blended with the flour-covered fat creates the steam that makes for the lightness of the crust. Chilling dough fifteen to twenty minutes before rolling tenderizes and, when baked in a hot oven, the coolness of the dough causes rapid air expansion contributing to its lightness.

Rolling. A pastry cloth and a stocking covered rolling pin are best for rolling but rolling out between two sheets of waxed paper can achieve the same result. This is preferable to rolling on a floured board which would add additional flour unnecessarily. Roll out from center lifting roller rather than rolling back and forth. Roll to ⅛-inch thickness or less, patching tears with scraps moistened with a little water. Roll two-inches larger than pie pan and either fold over to transfer to pan or roll loosely on roller and unroll onto pan. Shape to pan by working from outside edge towards center, lifting rather than stretching dough. Trim excess with sharp knife using a sawing motion. Prick bottom crust with fork to eliminate air pockets from forming during baking.

Flute edges high with extra dough for a one crust pie to hold in juices. For a lattice top, cut or pinch rolled out dough into ½-inch strips and weave about ¾-inches apart crimping loosely to edge moistened with water or milk. For fancy lattice, roll and twist strips before weaving. Roll solid crust tops ⅛-inch thick and one inch larger than pie pan. Cut fancy slashes or prick with fork to allow steam to escape during baking. Place on pie and tuck top edge under moistened bottom edge and pinch to seal.

Baking. Baking in a preheated oven using dark metal or ovenproof glass pie pans assures a golden crust. Shiny pie pans produce pale crusts. If crust is browning too quickly, cover with tin foil or with damp cloth and continue the baking.

Prebaked pie shells should be pricked with a fork and weighted with uncooked rice or beans to prevent the crust from heaving up and allow for even baking. Remove weights a few minutes before baking is completed. The top crust should be pricked and baked on a large cookie or baking sheet. Individual pie shells can be molded on upside down muffin tins or, for larger shells, use custard cups. When baking a meringue or custard pie in a prebaked shell, place pie pan inside second pie pan of the same size to prevent overbaking of crust.

Fruit fillings. Thicken acidy fruits with cornstarch, arrowroot or tapioca—acid may neutralize thickening power of flour. Let filling stand fifteen minutes and adjust sweetness before piling into pie. Juicier fillings may make bottom crust soggy. Try brushing bottom crust with melted butter or egg white to seal and heat filling before pouring into pie.

Meringue. Eggs should be at room temperature before using and don't separate and beat them until ready to use. The ratio of eggs to sugar is always the same (four egg whites to ½-T. sugar). Baking the meringue is for drying rather than for heating. Using bottom heat only, bake in a preheated oven; 225° F. for a soft, crunchy meringue; 275° F. for a chewier one. Many chefs preheat oven to 475° F., place pie in oven and turn off heat. Leave for eight hours without opening door. I would only recommend this to those of you with well insulated ovens.

Custards. Custard pies are best when eaten within three hours of cooking. Bacteria in the eggs grow rapidly and show no signs of spoilage. Custards can be refrigerated but often become watery. Custard pies call for prebaked crusts. Always have custard

THE DESSERT COOKBOOK

and shell cooled before assembling. You can bake custard in a pie pan of the same dimensions as the shell; then carefully slide custard into shell. Another method is to cook custard in a double boiler. When cooking custard has thickened, beat in saucepan until cooled (70° F.) allowing steam to escape. Steam thins the custard and causes it to "sweat."

Nine-inch pastry shell—single crust

1½ c. all-purpose flour
½ t. salt
½ c. shortening
1 egg yolk
4 to 5 T. ice water
2 t. lemon juice

Preheat oven to 450° F.

In large bowl, stir together flour and salt. Cut in shortening until pieces are size of small peas. Blend together egg yolk, 4 tablespoons ice water and lemon juice with fork. Add liquid to flour mixture, mixing lightly with fork until dough just sticks together. Add more water, if necessary. Press into a ball.

On pastry cloth or between 2 sheets waxed paper, rolling from center to edge, roll into ⅛-in. thick circle about 10-in. in diameter. Gently fit loosely into 9-in. pie pan. Trim edge and flute, as desired. Prick bottom and sides with fork.

If using metal pie pan, bake shell in oven until golden brown, 8 to 10 min. If using glass pie plate, bake shell at 425° F. Cool on wire rack.

Nine-inch pastry shell—double crust

2 c. all-purpose flour
½ t. salt
¾ c. shortening
2 egg yolks
6 to 8 T. ice water
1 T. lemon juice

In large bowl, stir together flour and salt. Cut in shortening until pieces are size of small peas. Blend together egg yolks, 6 tablespoons ice water and lemon juice with fork. Add liquid to flour mixture mixing lightly with fork until dough just sticks together. Add more water, if necessary. Press into a ball. Divide dough in half and shape each half into ball.

On pastry cloth or between 2 sheets waxed paper, roll one half, rolling from center to edge, into ⅛-in. thick circle about 10-in. in diameter. Gently fit pastry loosely into 9-in. pie plate or pan. Trim edge and brush with water. Fill pie as desired. Roll out remaining pastry as above and fit over filled pie. Trim ½ to 1-in. beyond plate edge. Tuck edge of top pastry under edge of bottom pastry. Press to seal and flute, as desired. Cut slits in top pastry to let steam escape. Bake as directed.

Graham cracker crust

1½ c. fine graham cracker crumbs (18 crackers)
¼ c. sugar
½ c. melted butter or margarine

Combine ingredients and mix well. Press firmly in unbuttered 9-in. pie plate. Bake in oven about 8 min. or until edge is lightly browned. Cool.

To make quick and easy crumbs, place crackers in blender for a few seconds.

Preheat oven to 375° F.

Cream cheese pastry

8 oz. sweet butter
8 oz. cream cheese
2 c. flour

Preheat oven to 450° F.

Cream the butter and cream cheese together with an electric beater until the mixture is well blended and creamy. Add the flour and mix with a wooden spoon until all flour has been absorbed, finishing the mixing with the hands if necessary. Form the pastry into a ball. Wrap it in plastic wrap and refrigerate it for 8 hours or overnight. Remove the pastry from the refrigerator 30 min. before you are ready to work with it.

Roll the pastry out thinly on a lightly floured board and arrange it in tart or pie pan(s). If it is to be baked empty, freeze it for 10 min. before baking. Bake for 5 min., then reduce the oven temperature to 400° F. Continue baking for 5 to 10 min. longer. Watch it carefully during the baking time, and quickly break any air bubbles with a fork as they form.

Makes two pie shells, or one 9-inch, two-crust pie.

Walnut or pecan pie shell

1 c. pecans or walnuts
1 T. sugar
¼ t. salt
1 T. (or more) butter

Blend the nuts and sugar in an electric blender or food processor until the nuts have been completely ground. Butter an 8-in. pie plate, using at least 1 tablespoon butter. Sprinkle in the nut mixture, distributing it evenly, and press it firmly into the butter. Bake for about 6 min. Cool on a wire rack.

Preheat oven to 400° F.

Makes one 8-inch shell.

Coconut crumb crust

1⅓ c. flaked coconut
2 T. melted butter
2 T. sugar
¼ c. arrowroot crumbs

Combine coconut and butter. Add sugar and crumbs, mixing thoroughly. Press firmly on bottom and sides of pie pan. Bake for 5 min. Cool thoroughly before filling. Good with all cream pies.

Makes one 9-inch single crust.

Preheat oven to 375° F.

Zwieback crust

1 c. zwieback crumbs
¼ c. confectioners' sugar
2 T. melted butter or margarine

Combine ingredients and press mixture in buttered 8-in. pie plate. Chill until set.

THE DESSERT COOKBOOK

Meringue for pies

for 9-in. pie
3 egg whites
¼ t. salt
¼ t. cream of tartar
⅓ c. sugar

Preheat oven to 350° F.

Beat egg whites until foamy. Add salt and cream of tartar. Beat until soft peaks form. Add sugar gradually, beating constantly; continue to beat until stiff peaks form. Pile meringue on warm pie filling. Spread onto crust edge to help prevent shrinking. Bake 15 to 20 min. until lightly browned.

Variation. For meringue shells, increase sugar in meringue recipe to ¾ cup. Shape into 6 mounds on heavy brown paper on baking sheet. Using back of spoon, form a hollow in the center of each mound. Bake at 275° F. for 1 hour. Turn off heat and let cool in oven. To serve, fill with fresh fruit or ice cream.

Apple crumb pie

5 to 7 tart apples, pared and sliced
1 unbaked 9-in. pastry shell
½ c. sugar
1 t. cinnamon
½ c. sugar
¾ c. enriched flour
⅓ c. butter or margarine

Preheat oven to 400° F.

Pare apples and cut in eighths. Arrange in unbaked pie shell. Mix ½ cup sugar with the cinnamon and sprinkle over apples.

Mix ½ cup sugar with the flour and cut in butter till crumbly. Sprinkle over apples. Bake in oven 40 min. or until done. Cool. Top with whipped cream and sprinkle with cinnamon-sugar mixture.

Makes one 9-inch pie.

Old-fashioned cherry pie

1 c. sugar
¼ c. all-purpose flour
¼ t. salt
3 c. drained, canned,
    pitted tart red
    cherries
½ c. juice from cherries
1 T. butter, softened
4 drops almond extract
pastry for 9-in. lattice-
    top pie

Combine sugar, flour, and salt then stir in juice. Cook and stir over medium heat until thick, then cook for 1 min. longer. Add cherries, butter and extract. Let stand while making pastry. Line 9-in. pie plate with pastry then pile with hot filling. Top with lattice crust and flute edges. Bake for 10 min. then reduce heat to 350° F. and bake another 45 min.

Makes one 9-inch pie.

Preheat oven to 450° F.

Blueberry cream cheese pie

1 crumb pie crust
1 (12-oz.) pkg. cream
    cheese
½ pt. sour cream
2 pts. fresh blueberries
2 T. sugar
⅓ c. water

Soften cream cheese and mix with sour cream. Spread on bottom and sides of pie shell. Wash and sort berries reserving ¾ cup. Pile rest of berries on cheese mixture in shell. Heat the ¾ cup berries in ⅓ cup water and 2 tablespoons sugar, until sugar dissolves. With back of wooden spoon gently mash the hot berries. Pour over the uncooked piled berries in shell. Chill several hours. May be served with unsweetened whipped cream.

Makes one 9-inch pie.

Strawberry-rhubarb pie

1 unbaked 9-in. pastry
shell

filling
5-6 c. strawberries
5-6 c. rhubarb,
(unpeeled)
4 T. flour
¾-1 c. sugar
1 T. butter

topping
1 c. all-purpose flour
1 c. dark brown sugar
½ c. butter
1½ t. cinnamon

Preheat oven to 450° F.

Prepare one 9-in. pie crust and mold into pie plate, making a slightly higher than usual fluted edge. Wash, hull and slice berries. Wash and dice rhubarb. Combine in bowl and sprinkle with flour and sugar. Stir gently and allow to stand 10 min. Prepare topping. Stir again and spoon into pie crust with slotted spoon, discarding any excess liquid. Dot with butter. Spread topping on pie. Place aluminum foil on middle shelf to catch any dripping. Bake for 10 min. Reduce heat to 350° F. and continue to bake for 30 or 40 min.

Work ingredients like pastry with pastry blender or two knives, but work quickly and lightly to prevent topping from becoming oily.

Makes one 9-inch pie.

Cranberry walnut pie

1½ c. cranberries
¼-½ c. sugar
¼-½ c. chopped walnuts
¼ c. butter, melted
½ c. sugar
½ c. flour
1 egg
ice cream

Preheat oven to 350° F.

Mix cranberries, sugar and walnuts pour into 9-in. pie plate. Combine butter, sugar, flour and egg thoroughly to form dough. Spread dough on top of cranberry mixture. Bake for 45 min. Serve warm with ice cream.

Makes one 9-inch pie.

Creamy peach pie

¾ c. sugar
¼ c. flour
¼ t. salt
¼ t. nutmeg
4 c. sliced and peeled
  peaches
1 unbaked 9-in. pie shell
½ c. heavy cream

In medium bowl mix sugar, flour, salt and nutmeg. Add to peaches and toss lightly. Turn into pie shell. Pour cream over top. Bake for 35-40 min. or until firm. Chill at least 2 hours.

Makes one 9-inch pie.

Preheat oven to 400° F.

Vanilla cream pie

1 baked 8-in. pastry
  shell, cooled
3 T. cornstarch
¼ c. sugar
½ t. salt
2 c. milk
2 egg yolks, beaten
2 T. butter or margarine
1 t. vanilla
½ c. whipping cream
1 T. confectioners' sugar

Mix cornstarch, sugar, and salt in heavy saucepan. Gradually stir in milk. Cook over moderate heat, stirring constantly, until thickened. Simmer 1 minute longer. Stir a little of the hot mixture into egg yolks; then stir yolks into remaining hot mixture. Cook 1 min. longer, stirring constantly. Stir in shortening and vanilla. Set saucepan in cold water to cool, stirring frequently. Change water occasionally.

Pour filling into pastry shell and chill thoroughly. Before serving, whip cream until stiff and beat in confectioners' sugar. Spread over pie.

Variations. For coconut cream pie, stir ½ to 1 cup shredded coconut, as desired, into the hot filling with shortening and vanilla.

For banana cream pie, slice 2 bananas into pie shell before adding filling.

For chocolate cream pie, increase sugar to ¾ cup. Cut 1½ ounces bitter chocolate into cream filling after adding milk.

Makes one 8-inch pie.

Fresh peach pie

1 unbaked 8-in. pie shell

filling
6-8 peaches, sliced
⅓ c. butter
1 c. sugar
1 egg, beaten
⅓ c. flour
1 t. vanilla

Put peaches in pie shell. Cream together butter and sugar. Add egg, flour and vanilla and mix well. Spread mixture over peaches. Bake about 1 hour or until thick in center.

Makes one 8-inch pie.

Preheat oven to 375° F.

Pecan pie

1 unbaked 9-in. pastry
   shell
1 c. pecan halves
3 eggs, beaten
½ c. sugar
1 c. dark corn syrup
¼ t. salt
1 t. vanilla
¼ c. melted butter or
   margarine

Spread nuts in bottom of pastry shell. Combine remaining ingredients and pour over nuts. Bake for 30 to 40 min., or until the filling appears set when the pie is gently moved.

Makes one 9-inch pie.

Preheat oven to 375° F.

Sour cream pie

pastry for 2-crust pie
1 c. sour cream
1 c. sugar
1 c. seeded raisins, cut
    fine
2 eggs
½ t. powdered
    cinnamon
½ t. powdered cloves
⅛ t. salt
2 T. vinegar

Beat the eggs. Mix the spices with the sugar, and add to the eggs with the raisins, cream, salt, and vinegar. Beat well. Pour the mixture into a deep, pastry-lined pie pan. Moisten the outer rim of the pastry, and press the top crust over the lower one to hold in the custard. Bake in oven 30 to 35 min. or until golden brown.

Makes one 9-inch deep dish pie.

Preheat oven to 350° F.

Lemon meringue pie

1 baked 9-in. pastry
    shell
1½ c. sugar
⅓ c. cornstarch
⅛ t. salt
1½ c. hot water
3 egg yolks, beaten
2 T. butter or margarine
1 t. lemon rind, grated
⅓ c. lemon juice
3 egg whites
1 t. lemon juice
⅓ c. sugar

Mix sugar, cornstarch, and salt in a saucepan. Gradually stir in hot water. Cook over medium heat, stirring constantly, until thickened, about 4 min. Cook 1 min. longer. Stir a little of the hot mixture into the egg yolks; then stir yolk mixture into remaining hot mixture. Cook 2 min. longer, stirring constantly. Overcooking may thin the mixture. Remove from heat. Stir in shortening, lemon rind, and ⅓ cup lemon juice. Pour warm filling into pastry shell. Beat egg whites with 1 teaspoon lemon juice until soft peaks form. Add ⅓ cup sugar gradually, beating constantly; continue beating to form stiff peaks. Pile meringue on cooled pie filling. Spread onto crust edge to help prevent shrinking. Bake 15 to 20 min. or until lightly browned.

Preheat oven to 225° F.   Makes one 9-inch pie.

Strawberry festival pie

1 baked 9-in. pie shell
2 pts. strawberries
   washed and hulled
1 c. sugar
2 env. unflavored gelatin
½ c. water
3 egg whites
1½ c. whipped cream

Wash, hull and slice 3 cups strawberries, saving remainder for garnish. Combine sliced strawberries and ½ cup sugar, let stand 5 min. then mash well.

Soften gelatin in water in saucepan, heat slowly until dissolved. Cool slightly, stir into strawberry mixture. Place bowl in a pan of ice water, chill stirring occasionally until mixture is as thick as unbeaten egg white. Don't overchill.

Beat egg whites until foamy, add remaining ½ cup sugar, 1 tablespoon at a time until meringue holds firm peaks.

Fold meringue, then 1 cup whipped cream into strawberry mixture. Pour into baked pie shell. Garnish with extra berries and remainder of whipped cream.

Makes one 9-inch pie.

Lemon chiffon pie

1 baked 9-in. graham
   cracker pie crust
4 eggs, separated
1 env. unflavored gelatin
½ c. sugar
⅛ t. salt
⅔ c. fresh lemon juice
4 T. water
1 t. grated lemon rind

Mix gelatin, sugar, salt, water, lemon juice in saucepan. Add egg yolks, beat until well blended. Cook and stir over low heat until gelatin dissolves, about 5 min.

Add lemon rind, chill until mixture begins to thicken. Beat egg whites and ½ cup sugar (or less) until stiff. Fold in gelatin mixture, pour into cool pie shell and chill. Just before serving, top with slightly sweetened whipped cream and dash of nutmeg.

Makes one 9-inch pie.

Chocolate chip pecan pie

1 unbaked 9-in. pie shell
3 eggs, slightly beaten
1¼ c. corn syrup
⅛ t. salt
1 t. vanilla
½ c. sugar
½ c. pecan halves
1 c. (6-oz.) semi-sweet
    chocolate chips
1 c. whipped cream

Combine eggs, corn syrup, salt, vanilla and sugar in a large bowl. Mix well, then stir in pecans and chocolate chips.

Pour into unbaked pie shell. Bake for about 55 min. or until pie is set. Cool. Spread whipped cream on pie.

Makes one 9-inch pie.

Preheat oven to 375° F.

Raspberry parfait pie

1 (10-oz.) pkg. butter
    cookies
2 T. melted butter
1 (6-oz.) pkg. frozen
    raspberries
1 (3-oz.) pkg. raspberry
    gelatin
1 pt. vanilla ice cream

Press crushed cookies blended with butter into 9-in. pie pan. Thaw raspberries. Drain juice and add enough water to make 1 cup. Boil liquid and dissolve gelatin in it. Stir in chunked ice cream. Stir until dissolved. Fold in raspberries. Chill about 10 min. until slightly thickened. Pour into crust and chill several hours.

Makes one 9-inch pie.

Chocolate angel pie

2 egg whites
⅛ t. salt
⅛ t. cream of tartar
½ c. sifted sugar
½ c. pecans, finely
  chopped
½ t. vanilla
1 pkg. German sweet
  chocolate
3 T. water
1½ t. vanilla
1 c. whipped cream

Beat egg whites with salt and cream of tartar until foamy. Add sugar slowly, beating until stiff peaks are formed.

Fold in nuts and ½ teaspoon vanilla. Spread in greased 8-in. pie pan. Build up sides ½-in. above pan. Cook for 50 to 55 min. Cool.

Melt chocolate and water over low heat, stirring constantly. Cool until thick. Add 1 teaspoon vanilla, fold in whipped cream. Pile the chocolate mixture into meringue shell. Chill 2 hours.

Makes one 8-inch pie.

Preheat oven to 300° F.

Lemon chess pie

¾ c. butter
1 c. sugar
5 egg yolks
juice of 3 lemons
grated rind of 2 lemons
5 egg whites, beaten
1 unbaked 9-in. pie shell

Cream the butter and sugar Add the egg yolks and beat. Add the lemon juice and rind. Fold in the egg whites. Pour into unbaked pie shell. Bake for 30 min. or until slightly brown.

Makes one 9-inch pie.

Preheat oven to 325° F.

Pumpkin custard pie

1 can (16-oz.) solid
   pack pumpkin or 2 c.
   mashed, cooked
   pumpkin
¾ c. sugar
½ t. salt
2 t. cinnamon
½ t. ginger
⅛ t. cloves
3 eggs, slightly beaten
1 can (13-oz.)
   evaporated milk
1 unbaked 9-in. pie shell
1 c. whipped cream

Blend together pumpkin, sugar, salt and spices. Stir in eggs and evaporated milk until well blended. Pour into unbaked pie shell.

Bake in oven until knife inserted near center comes out clean, 50 to 55 min. Cool on wire rack. Garnish with whipped cream.

Makes one 9-in. pie.

Preheat oven to 350° F.

French silk pie

¾ c. sugar
½ c. butter, softened
2 (1-oz.) squares
   unsweetened
   chocolate, melted
1 t. vanilla
4 eggs
1 baked 9-in. pie shell
¼ c. slivered almonds,
   toasted
½ square (½-oz.)
   unsweetened
   chocolate, shaved

In small mixing bowl beat together sugar and butter at medium speed until creamy and fluffy. Blend in melted chocolate and vanilla. Add eggs, one at a time, beating at high speed about 3 min. after each addition. Pour into baked pie shell. Sprinkle almonds around outer edge and arrange shaved chocolate in center of filling. Chill at least 2 hours.

Makes one 9-in. pie.

THE DESSERT COOKBOOK

Rhubarb custard pie

pastry for 2-crust pie
1¼ c. sugar
¼ c. all-purpose flour
¼ t. salt
4 c. (about 1 lb.) diced
  fresh rhubarb*
3 eggs
½ t. vanilla
2 T. butter

Preheat oven to 425° F.

Divide pastry in half; roll each half into circle ⅛ inch thick. Line 9-inch pie plate with one half. Trim edge.

In large bowl, combine sugar, flour and salt. Stir in rhubarb, coating evenly. Spread rhubarb mixture evenly in pie shell. Beat together eggs and vanilla and pour over rhubarb. Dot with butter. Moisten edge of pastry and cover with remaining pastry. Cut slits in top to allow steam to escape. Trim, seal and flute edges as desired.

Bake in oven 15 min. Reduce heat to 350° F. and bake until knife inserted in center comes out clean, 30 minutes longer. Cool on wire rack. Serve warm or cold.

*2 packages (1 lb. each) frozen, unsweetened cut rhubarb, thawed and well drained, may be substituted for fresh rhubarb. Reduce sugar to ¾ cup.

Makes one 9-inch pie.

Pineapple pie

pastry for 2-crust pie
2 c. sliced pineapple
¾ c. sugar
2 T. lemon juice
1 T. flour
½ t. nutmeg
1 t. cinnamon

Mix sugar, spices and flour together. Add lemon and pineapple. Pile into pie shell and dot with butter. Add top crust. Bake 45 to 50 min.

Makes one 9-inch pie.

Preheat oven to 350° F.

Banana cream pie

½ c. sugar
¼ t. salt
⅓ c. flour
1⅓ c. milk
¾ c. water
3 egg yolks
1 c. bananas, thinly
  sliced
1 baked 9-in. pie shell
3 egg whites
⅓ c. sugar
½ t. baking powder

Combine sugar, salt, flour, milk and water over low heat. Add small amount of this mixture to egg yolks, mix, and pour back into custard. Cook 3-4 min. longer. Add bananas and pour into baked pie shell. Top with meringue made of 3 egg whites, ⅓ cup sugar, and ½ teaspoon baking powder, beaten until stiff. Spoon over pie and bake until lightly browned. Pineapple cream pie can be made in the same manner by substituting 1 cup chopped pineapple for the bananas.

Makes one 9-inch pie.

Preheat oven to 225° F.

Hawaiian banana pie

4 c. sliced bananas, ripe
  but firm
½ c. pineapple juice
½ c. sugar
1 t. cinnamon
1 T. butter or margarine
pastry for 2 crust pie

Soak sliced bananas in pineapple juice for 20 to 30 min. Drain, saving the juice. Place bananas in pastry lined 9-in. pie pan, add sugar and cinnamon which have been mixed together. Add 2 tablespoons of the pineapple juice. Dot with butter and cover with top crust. Bake for 30 to 45 min., or until crust is browned.

Makes one 9-inch pie.

Preheat oven to 400° F.

Maple apple pie

pastry for 2-crust pie
5 c. apples
1 c. maple syrup
2 T. flour
1 t. cinnamon
1½ t. salt
2 T. butter or margarine
milk

Preheat oven to 425° F.

Fit bottom pie crust in 9-in. pie pan. Pare and slice apples and put in pan. Mix syrup, flour, cinnamon and salt. Pour over apples. Dot with butter. Cover with top pie crust. Seal moistened edges of crust together. Cut a few slits in top and brush with milk.

Bake about 50 min., or until browned and apples are tender.

Makes one 9-inch pie.

Apple chiffon pie

crust
⅓ c. butter or
   margarine
2 T. sugar
1¼ c. graham cracker
   crumbs

filling
3 egg yolks, slightly
   beaten
⅓ c. apple cider
1 T. lemon juice
1 t. lemon rind, grated
2 T. sugar
1 T. unflavored gelatin
¼ c. cold water
2 c. apples, pared,
   shredded
3 egg whites
¼ t. salt
¼ c. sugar
nutmeg (optional)

To make crust, stir shortening and 2 tablespoons sugar together in a saucepan over low heat until shortening is melted. Mix in cracker crumbs. Press evenly into a 9-in. pie pan and chill.

To make filling, mix egg yolks, cider, lemon juice, lemon rind, and 2 tablespoons sugar. Cook over low heat, stirring constantly, until mixture begins to thicken, about 2 min. Sprinkle gelatin on water and let stand a few min. Add gelatin to hot mixture; stir until dissolved. Cool until thick but not set. Pare and shred apples, mix into gelatin mixture immediately. Beat egg whites until foamy. Add salt and beat until soft peaks form. Slowly add remaining sugar, beating constantly until stiff. Fold into apple mixture. Pour into graham cracker shell. Sprinkle with nutmeg as desired. Chill until firm.

Makes one 9-inch pie.

Cherry crumb pie

1 unbaked 9-in. pie
   crust
2 (16-oz.) cans red,
   sour, pitted cherries
¾ c. sugar
¼ c. cornstarch
¼ t. salt
1 c. cherry liquid
¼ t. almond extract
⅓ c. brown sugar,
   packed
⅔ c. flour, unsifted
¼ c. butter or
   margarine

Drain cherries; save liquid. Mix sugar, cornstarch, and salt in a saucepan. Add cherry liquid; stir until smooth. Cook over medium heat, stirring constantly, until thickened. Remove from heat; add cherries and almond extract. Pour into pastry shell. Mix brown sugar and flour. Mix in shortening until mixture is crumbly. Sprinkle brown sugar mixture over the cherries. Bake 40 to 45 min. or until crust and topping are lightly browned.

Makes one 9-inch pie.

Preheat oven to 400° F.

Fresh blueberry pie

pastry for 2-crust pie
4 c. fresh blueberries
¾ to 1 c. sugar
3 T. flour
½ t. grated lemon peel
dash salt
½ t. cinnamon
½ t. nutmeg

Line 9-in. pie plate with pastry. Combine remaining ingredients and fill pie shell. Sprinkle with 1 to 2 teaspoons lemon juice and dot with 1 tablespoon butter. Adjust top crust. Bake 35 to 40 min. Serve warm.

Makes one 9-inch pie

Preheat oven to 400° F.

Pumpkin pie

1 unbaked 9-in. pie shell
1½ c. cooked or canned
   pumpkin
¼ c. white corn syrup
2 eggs
½ c. evaporated milk
2 T. butter or margarine
½ c. hot milk
½ c. brown sugar, firmly
   packed
½ t. salt
1½ t. cinnamon
½ t. nutmeg
¼ t. ginger
⅛ t. cloves
1 c. whipped cream

Preheat oven to 425° F.

Combine pumpkin, corn syrup, eggs and evaporated milk. Stir butter into hot milk. Combine brown sugar, salt and spices. Mix until well blended. Combine all three mixtures; pour into pastry-lined pie pan. Bake for 15 min., then reduce heat to 350° F. and bake 35 min. longer or until knife inserted comes out clean. Just before serving, garnish with dollops of whipped cream.

Makes one 9-in. pie.

Fruit delight pie

1 9-in. graham cracker
   crust
2 c. whipped cream
1 pkg. (8-oz.) cream
   cheese, softened
¼ c. confectioners'
   sugar
¼ t. vanilla
½ c. chopped pecans
1 c. canned blueberry,
   peach, or cherry pie
   filling

Make graham cracker crust. Beat cream cheese, sugar, and vanilla into whipped cream until smooth. Stir in nuts. Pour into pie shell. Top with pie filling. Chill at least 3 hours before serving.

Makes one 9-inch pie.

French apple pie

pastry for 2-crust pie
6 c. tart apples, pared
   and sliced
½ c. raisins
⅔ c. granulated sugar
1 T. cornstarch
½ t. cinnamon
1 T. lemon juice
½ c. confectioners'
   sugar
1½ to 2 T. water

Pare, slice and spread apples into pie shell. Mix raisins, granulated sugar, cornstarch, and cinnamon and sprinkle over apples. Drizzle lemon juice over apple mixture. Top with second crust. Fold edges of pastry under, moisten and press together firmly to seal. Bake 45 to 60 min., or until the apples are tender when pierced with a knife and the crust is lightly browned. Cool pie. Mix confectioner's sugar and water to make a thick but spreadable frosting. Spread on slightly warm pie.

Makes one 9-inch pie.

Preheat oven to 400° F.

Deep-dish apple pie

filling
9 to 12 apples
1½ c. sugar
½ t. cinnamon
½ t. nutmeg
dash of mace
¾ t. salt
3 T. butter or margarine

pastry
1½ c. sifted flour
½ c. shortening
3 T. cold milk
cream

Peel and slice apples to fill 12x8x2-in. baking dish. Combine sugar, spices and ¼ teaspoon salt; sprinkle over apples, mixing lightly. Dot with butter.

Sift together flour and ½ teaspoon salt; cut in shortening until pieces are size of small peas. Add milk by teaspoonfuls, tossing with fork until mixture is just dampened.

Turn mixture onto square of waxed paper; gather up corners, pressing from outside to form compact ball. Roll out about ⅛-in. thick between two sheets of waxed paper; place over apples. Brush with cream; cut steam vents.

Bake in oven for 15 min.; reduce heat to 350° F. and bake 45 min. longer.

Preheat oven to 450° F.

Makes 8 to 10 servings.

Favorite apple pie

6 large tart apples
pastry for 2-crust pie
2 T. flour
½ c. granulated sugar
½ c. brown sugar, firmly
  packed
¾ t. cinnamon
¼ t. nutmeg
⅛ t. ginger
⅛ t. salt
1 T. lemon juice
3 T. butter or margarine

Peel and quarter apples into saucepan. Add ¼ cup cold water; simmer until tender, about 5 min. Cool.

Line 9-in. pie pan with ½ pastry; fill with apples.

Combine remaining ingredients, except butter; sprinkle over apples; dot with butter. Moisten edges of undercrust.

Adjust top crust with 6 vents; trim and seal edges.

Bake in oven for 10 min.; reduce heat to 350° F. and bake 45 min. longer.

Makes one 9-in. pie.

Preheat oven to 450° F.

Glazed apple-raisin pie

pastry for 2-crust pie
¾ c. sugar
2 T. flour
⅛ t. salt
½ t. cinnamon
6 c. peeled, sliced tart
  apples
½ c. seedless raisins
2 T. orange juice
3 T. butter or margarine

Divide pastry in 2 parts; roll out half to line 9-in. pie pan.

Combine sugar, flour, salt and cinnamon; mix with apples and raisins; place in pie pan. Sprinkle with orange juice; dot with butter.

Cover with top crust; seal edges. Bake in oven 15 min.; reduce heat to 350° F. and bake 40 min. longer.

For confectioners' sugar glaze, mix together 1 cup sugar, 3 tablespoons strained orange juice and 1 teaspoon grated orange rind. Spread over hot pie.

Makes one 9-inch pie.

Preheat oven to 400° F.

Honey cheese pie

1 baked 9-in. pie shell
1 lb. ricotta cheese
¼ c. sugar
½ c. honey
3 eggs
2 grated zest of lemon

Preheat oven to 350° F.

Combine the ricotta cheese with ¼ cup sugar. Add the honey and mix well. Beat the eggs lightly and add them to the cheese mixture Stir in the lemon zest. Pour into the pie shell. Bake for 45 min., or until lightly browned. Serve it warm or chilled.

Makes one 9-inch pie.

Pumpkin chiffon pie

1 env. unflavored gelatin
¾ c. firmly packed
   brown sugar
½ t. salt
½ t. ginger
½ t. cinnamon
¼ t. nutmeg
4 eggs, separated
½ c. light cream
¼ c. water
1 can (16-oz.) solid
   pack pumpkin or 2 c.
   mashed, cooked
   pumpkin
¼ t. cream of tartar
¼ c. sugar
1 baked 9-in. pie shell
½ c. whipped cream

In medium saucepan, stir together gelatin, brown sugar, salt and spices. Beat together egg yolks, cream and water until blended. Stir yolk mixture into gelatin mixture. Cook, stirring constantly, over low heat until gelatin dissolves completely and mixture thickens slightly, about 5 to 8 min. Remove from heat. Thoroughly blend in pumpkin. Chill, stirring occasionally, until mixture mounds slightly when dropped from a spoon, 30 to 45 min.

Wash and dry beaters. In large mixing bowl beat egg whites and cream of tartar at high speed until foamy. Add ¼ cup sugar, 1 tablespoon at a time, beating constantly until sugar is dissolved and whites are glossy and stand in soft peaks. Fold chilled pumpkin mixture into egg whites. Pile mixture into pie shell. Chill until firm, at least 3 hours. Garnish with whipped cream.

Makes one 9-inch pie.

Chocolate chiffon pie

4 eggs, separated
2 (1-oz.) squares
  unsweetened
  chocolate
1¼ c. milk
1 env. unflavored gelatin
1 c. sugar, divided
¼ t. salt
1 t. vanilla
¼ t. cream of tartar
1 baked 9-in. pie shell
  or graham cracker
  crumb crust
½ c. whipped cream
½ square (½-oz.)
  unsweetened
  chocolate, shaved

In small mixing bowl, beat egg yolks at high speed until thick and lemon-colored, about 5 min. Set aside.

In small saucepan melt 2 squares chocolate over low heat. Gradually blend in milk. Stir in gelatin, ½ cup sugar and salt. Let stand 1 min. Blend in beaten yolks. Cook, stirring constantly, over medium heat until mixture thickens slightly, about 10 min. Stir in vanilla. Chill, stirring occasionally, until mixture mounds slightly when dropped from a spoon, 30 to 45 min.

Wash and dry beaters. In large mixing bowl, beat egg whites and cream of tartar at high speed until foamy. Add remaining ½ cup sugar, 1 tablespoon at a time, beating constantly until sugar is dissolved and whites are glossy and stand in soft peaks. Gently but thoroughly fold chilled chocolate mixture into egg whites. Pile mixture into pie shell. Chill until firm, at least 3 hours. Garnish with whippped cream and shaved chocolate.

Makes one 9-inch pie.

Orange chiffon pie

4 eggs, separated
1 env. unflavored gelatin
¾ c. sugar
½ c. orange juice
¼ t. salt
2 T. lemon juice
2 t. grated orange peel
¼ t. cream of tartar
1 c. whipped cream
1 (9-in.) graham cracker
  crumb crust
orange slices

In small mixing bowl beat egg yolks at high speed until thick and lemon-colored, about 5 min.

In medium saucepan, combine gelatin, ¼ cup sugar, orange juice and salt. Let stand 1 min. Gradually stir in beaten yolks. Cook, stirring constantly, over medium heat until mixture thickens slightly, about 5 min. Remove from heat and stir in lemon juice and orange peel. Chill, stirring occasionally, until mixture mounds slightly when dropped from a spoon, 30 to 45 min.

Wash and dry beaters. In large mixing bowl, beat egg whites and cream of tartar at high speed until foamy. Add remaining ½ cup sugar, one tablespoon at a time, beating constantly until sugar is dissolved and whites are glossy and stand in soft peaks. Fold chilled yolk mixture and whipped cream into egg whites. Pile mixture into crust. Chill until firm, at least 3 hours. Garnish with orange slices.

Makes one 9-inch pie.

Kitty Bob's mud pie

1 pkg. chocolate wafers
1 stick unsalted butter
2 qt. coffee ice cream
slivered almonds

chocolate sauce
6-oz. semi-sweet
  chocolate, broken up
½ c. water
2 T. instant coffee
1 t. sugar
10 T. sweet butter

Crush wafers and melt butter. Mix together and press mixture into buttered 9-in. pie pan. Place in freezer for 20 min. Make chocolate sauce by combining chocolate, water, coffee, and sugar over low heat. When chocolate is melted, add butter in small pieces, and stir until melted. Cool until the mixture can be easily spread. Remove the pie pan from freezer, spread ice cream over the crust, and top with chocolate sauce. Sprinkle with the nuts.

Makes one 9-in. pie.

Coconut cream pie

1 c. sugar
3 T. cornstarch
¼ t. salt
3 eggs, separated
2 c. milk
1 c. flaked coconut
2 T. butter
1½ t. vanilla
¼ t. cream of tartar
1 baked 9-in. pie shell

Preheat oven to 350° F.

In medium saucepan combine ⅔ cup sugar, cornstarch and salt. In bowl beat together egg yolks and milk until blended. Gradually stir milk mixture into sugar mixture. Cook over medium heat, stirring constantly, until mixture thickens and bubbles. Boil, stirring constantly, 1 min. Remove from heat. Stir in ¾ cup coconut, butter and 1 teaspoon vanilla. Pour into baked pie shell. Set aside.

In large mixing bowl, beat egg whites and cream of tartar at high speed until foamy. Add remaining ⅓ cup sugar, 1 tablespoon at a time, beating constantly until sugar is dissolved and whites are glossy and stand in soft peaks. Beat in remaining ½ teaspoon vanilla.

Spread meringue over filling, starting with small amounts at edges and sealing to crust all around. Cover pie with remaining meringue, spreading evenly in attractive swirls. Sprinkle with remaining ¼ cup coconut.

Bake in oven until peaks are lightly browned, 12 to 15 min. Cool to room temperature.

Makes one 9-inch pie.

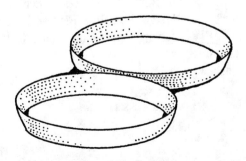

Nesselrode pie

1 env. unflavored gelatin
¾ c. sugar, divided
¼ t. salt
1 c. milk
4 eggs, separated
3 T. brandy
¼ t. cream of tartar
¼ t. vanilla
1 c. diced candied fruit, divided
1 (9-in.) graham cracker crumb crust

In medium saucepan, combine gelatin, ½ cup sugar and salt. Stir in ½ cup milk and let stand 1 min. Beat together egg yolks and remaining milk. Stir yolk mixture into gelatin mixture. Cook, stirring constantly, over medium heat until mixture thickens and coats a metal spoon, about 6 to 8 min. Remove from heat. Stir in brandy. Chill, stirring occasionally, until mixture mounds slightly when dropped from a spoon, 30 to 45 min.

In large mixing bowl, beat egg whites and cream of tartar at high speed until foamy. Add remaining ¼ cup sugar, 1 tablespoon at a time, beating constantly until sugar is dissolved and whites are glossy and stand in soft peaks. Beat in vanilla.

Gently fold ¾ cup candied fruit into chilled gelatin mixture. Fold gelatin-fruit mixture into egg whites. Pile into crust. Garnish with remaining ¼ cup fruit. Chill until firm, at least 3 hours or overnight.

Makes one 9-inch pie.

Fudge sundae pie

1 c. evaporated milk
1 pkg. semi-sweet chocolate chips (6-oz.)
1 c. miniature marshmallows
¼ t. salt
1 pkg. vanilla wafers (12-oz.)
1 qt. vanilla ice cream
pecan halves or cashews

In top of double boiler, combine milk, chocolate, marshmallows, and salt. Stir over medium heat until the chocolate and marshmallows are melted and mixture is thick. Cool to spreading consistency. Line 9-in. pie pan with vanilla wafers. Spoon half of ice cream over wafers, and spread half of chocolate mixture over ice cream. Repeat and top with nuts. Freeze until firm. Remove from freezer 20 min. before serving. Use a knife dipped in hot water to cut into wedges.

Makes 6 servings.

Key lime pie

4 eggs, separated
1 can (14-oz.)
   sweetened, condensed
   milk
⅓ c. lime juice
1½ t. grated lime peel
1 (9-in.) graham cracker
   crumb crust
¼ t. cream of tartar
¼ c. sugar

Preheat oven to 350° F.

In small mixing bowl, beat egg yolks. Blend in condensed milk, lime juice and peel. Pour into crust.

In large mixing bowl, beat egg whites and cream of tartar at high speed until foamy. Add sugar, 1 tablespoon at a time, beating constantly until sugar is dissolved and whites are glossy and stand in soft peaks.

Spread meringue over filling, starting with small amounts at edges and sealing to crust all around. Cover pie with remaining meringue, spreading evenly in attractive swirls.

Bake in oven until peaks are lightly browned, 12 to 15 min. Cool to room temperature.

Makes one 9-inch pie.

Ice cream pie

1 pkg. semi-sweet
   chocolate chips
   (6-oz.)
2 T. butter
2 c. crispy rice cereal
1 qt. ice cream, softened
   to spreading
   consistency

In the top of a double boiler, melt chocolate chips and butter. Add cereal, stirring to make sure all the cereal is coated with chocolate. Pour into a 9-in. pie pan. With the back of a spoon, shape mixture to the pan. Mound ice cream on top. Try a variety of ice cream flavors—chocolate, mint, coffee, peppermint, or toasted almond. Freeze until ready to serve. Remove from freezer 15 min. before serving.

Makes 6 to 8 servings.

Cranberry delight

3 c. chopped apples
2 c. raw cranberries
1 c. sugar
1½ c. quick-cooking
    oats
½ c. brown sugar
⅓ c. flour
¾ t. salt
½ c. melted butter
½ c. chopped walnuts

Combine apples, raw cranberries, and sugar. Place in 9-in. unbaked pie shell. Combine oats, brown sugar, flour, salt, and melted butter. Mix until crumbly, sprinkle over fruit. Sprinkle chopped walnuts on top. Bake for 1 hour.

Makes one 9-inch pie.

Preheat oven to 350° F.

Hard meringues

The egg beater was invented in 1870. In earlier times, the transformation of egg whites to meringue was a major undertaking, but good cooks considered it worth the effort. Hard meringues were and are the basis of many culinary triumphs including tortes, fruit and frozen desserts.

4 egg whites
½ t. cream of tartar
½ t. salt
1 c. sugar

Preheat oven to 250° F.

Beat egg whites, cream of tartar, and salt at high speed until foamy. Add sugar, 2 tablespoonfuls at a time, beating constantly until sugar is dissolved* and whites are glossy and stand in soft peaks.

Place several layers of ungreased paper on a cookie sheet. Using ⅓ cup meringue for each, shape into "nests" with a spoon. Make each meringue about 3-in. wide, and build up an edge to form a rim. Flute rims if desired.

Bake in preheated oven until firm and delicately browned, about 50 min. Turn off oven. Leave meringues in oven with door closed for 1 hour.

*Rub just a bit of meringue between thumb and forefinger to feel if sugar has dissolved.

Makes 1 dozen.

Meringue shell

3 egg whites
1 t. vanilla
¼ t. cream of tartar
dash of salt
1 c. sugar

Preheat oven to 275° F.

Have egg whites at room temperature. Add vanilla, cream of tartar, and salt. Beat till frothy. Gradually add sugar, a small amount at a time, beating until very stiff peaks form and sugar is dissolved.

Cover cookie sheet with plain ungreased paper. Using a 9-in. round cake pan as guide, draw a circle on the paper. Spread meringue over circle; shape into shell with back of spoon. Make the bottom ½-in. thick, the sides 1¾-in. high. Bake in very slow oven for 1 hour. Turn off heat and let the meringue dry in oven (door closed) at least 2 hours.

To make a pretty meringue shell, ripple the edges before baking.

Individual meringue shells. Make meringue as above. Cover cookie sheet with plain ungreased paper. Draw eight 3½-in. circles; spread each with about ⅓ cup meringue. Shape with spoon to make shells. Bake in very slow oven (275° F.) 1 hour. For crisper meringues, turn off heat; let dry in oven (door closed) about 1 hour.

THE DESSERT COOKBOOK

Princess Ann tart

crust
½ c. flour
1 t. baking powder
2 T. sugar
pinch of salt
6 T. butter
2 T. cold water
1 jar raspberry jam
    (8-oz.)

To make the crust, combine flour, baking powder, sugar, and salt. Work in butter until mixture resembles cornmeal. Add water and stir into stiff dough. Roll out dough on a floured surface. Place dough in 9-in. pie pan. Spread the raspberry jam in the bottom crust. It may need to be melted.

custard
2 egg yolks
1 c. milk
1 T. sugar
1 t. flour
pinch of salt
1 t. vanilla

To make the custard, combine all ingredients and beat well. Pour into prepared crust. Bake for 30 min. While the custard is baking, prepare the meringue.

meringue
2 egg whites
4 T. sugar
¼ t. cream of tartar

To make the meringue, beat egg whites and cream of tartar until soft peaks form. Add sugar gradually while beating. Beat until stiff peaks form. After the custard has been cooked and cooled, pile on the meringue and bake at 375° F. until golden-brown, 5 to 10 min.

Preheat oven to 350° F.   Makes 6 to 8 servings.

Sour cream cherry tart

2 c. sifted flour
¼ t. baking powder
½ t. salt
2 T. sugar
½ c. butter or
  margarine
½ t. cinnamon
¾ c. sugar
2 cans pitted sour
  cherries, drained
  (1 lb. each)
½ t. almond extract
1 beaten egg
1 c. sour cream

Combine first four ingredients. Cut in shortening until consistency of cornmeal. Press evenly on bottom and sides of the prepared pan. Gently mix extract and cherries and spoon over flour mixture. Sprinkle ¾ cup sugar mixed with cinnamon on top. Bake for 15 min. Mix egg and sour cream. Spoon over cherries and bake 30 min. longer. Serve warm or cool.

Makes one 8-in. tart.

Preheat oven to 400° F.
Grease an 8x8-in. pan.

Pumpkin tarts

1 T. cornstarch
¾ c. sugar
½ t. cinnamon
¼ t. ginger
2 egg yolks, slightly
  beaten
1 c. milk
¾ c. cooked or canned
  pumpkin
2 egg whites, stiffly
  beaten
½ c. heavy cream,
  whipped
⅓ c. chopped pecans
8 small tart shells

Mix cornstarch, sugar, cinnamon, and ginger. Stir in egg yolks and milk. Cook in double boiler over hot water until thickened, stirring constantly. Add pumpkin. Freeze.

Break into chunks; put chunks in a bowl. Beat until smooth with rotary beater. This extra beating adds air and makes a smoother ice cream. Fold in egg whites, whipped cream, and nuts. Pour into 8 shells and freeze until firm.

Makes 8 servings.

Tiny fudge tarts

1½ c. all-purpose flour
¼ t. salt
½ c. butter or
   margarine
3 T. water
1 t. vanilla

Mix flour and salt; cut in butter. Sprinkle with water and vanilla; mix well with fork. Using ½ of dough at a time, roll out 1/16-in. thick on cloth-covered board generously sprinkled with sugar. Cut in 2½-in. squares. Spread 1 level teaspoon filling in center of each square. Bring corners to center; moisten with water to seal. Place sealed side up or down on ungreased baking sheet. Bake 15 to 20 min.

fudge filling
½ c. butter or
   margarine
1 egg yolk
½ c. sugar
1 t. vanilla
¼ c. cocoa
½ c. chopped nuts or
   flaked coconut

Mix ingredients thoroughly.

Makes 2½ dozen tarts.

Preheat oven to 350° F.

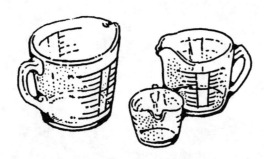

Cakes, tortes, and frostings

Cakes, tortes, and frostings

Cakes can generally be divided into two categories; those that depend solely upon eggs for leavening and those that use chemical leavening and shortening. The exceptions are pound cake and chiffon cake which are rich, moist mixtures leavened by eggs but contain a large proportion of shortening. Sponge cakes are often made with whole eggs, angel food cakes depend upon only the whites, while chiffon cakes (and some pound cakes) derive height from the use of separated eggs. Chemically leavened cakes also contain shortening (usually butter for best flavor), are finely grained, east to frost and are most often used as layer cakes. Tortes are light but rich mixtures that usually use separated eggs and ground nuts to replace some or all of the flour. They may be filled but often need little more than a dusting of powdered sugar or a dollop of whipped cream as a finishing touch. Tortes keep better than any other kind of cake.

The best cakes have a good, moist crumb, are even textured and have a delicate flavor. This balance depends entirely upon the quality of ingredients and accurate measurement. Have all ingredients at room temperature before you start. Measure dry ingredients by lightly dipping in the spoon or cup, then sweeping off the top to make a level measurement. Determine liquid measurement with an appropriate cup, and gauge at eye level. Preheat the oven at least ten minutes ahead. Prepare and use the correct size pans as the recipe directs and never fill a pan more than two-thirds full in order to allow for expansion. Glass, ceramic or black steel pans retain more heat and thus require a 25° lower oven temperature in most cases. Cakes should be baked in the center of an oven allowing plenty of room for air circulation. If you must use two racks, stagger the pans so one will not cover the other. Do not test a cake until five to ten minutes before the baking time is up. Most cakes are done when a wooden pick or thin skewer inserted off center comes out clean and the top springs back when lightly pressed with the fingertips. Cakes should be allowed to cool about five minutes in the pan before being turned out onto a rack to cool. This permits the cake to shrink a bit and make for easier removal. Sponge, chiffon and angel food cakes should be inverted and suspended to allow air circulation; and then cooled completely in the pan. Do not attempt to frost or fill a cake that is not completely cooled. In fact, cakes may ice better if they are first popped into the freezer for about thirty minutes.

In general, light chiffon or sponge cakes can handle buttery frostings while dense poundcakes or fruit and nut cakes need little or no enhancement at all. Buttercream iced cakes freeze quite successfully, but those frosted with custards or whipped cream should be frozen unfrosted for best results. Cakes with little or no shortening are best eaten on the day they are baked while poundcakes, fruitcakes and some tortes are even better on the second day.

For best success in cake baking, do not make substitutions of any major ingredients since a chemical or dry/liquid imbalance can dramatically alter the finished product.

Angel and sponge cakes

Read recipes carefully. Assemble all ingredients, use standard measuring utensils, and measure accurately.

Prepare pans according to directions in recipe. *Do not grease.*

Spread mixed batter to sides of pan and fill all corners. Angel and sponge cakes are done when they spring back to the touch. Invert in pan; cool thoroughly.

If cake falls away from the pan, it may be because the pan was greased or because of insufficient baking.

If you want a brown crust, remove cake from pan as soon as it is cool. The longer you keep cool sponge cakes in the pan, the more crust will adhere to the pan.

Angel cakes

Angel cakes are leavened only with air. Whether or not you get a light tender cake depends on how much you beat the egg whites, the lightness with which you fold in the sugar and flour mixture, and the temperature at which you bake the cake.

Sift half the sugar with the flour 4 times. Add salt, flavorings, and cream of tartar to egg whites. Beat until egg whites are stiff enough to hold up in soft peaks, but are still moist and glossy. Beat in half the sugar, 2 tablespoons at a time. This step brings sugar into solution and prepares the foam for taking the flour smoothly. Remember to use very fine granulated sugar because it dissolves faster and easier and gives a cake with a finer texture.

Sift flour-and-sugar mixture in quarters over the beaten egg whites. Fold in lightly with a down-up-and-over motion, turning the bowl gradually.

Sponge cakes

Methods for making sponge cakes vary from recipe to recipe, but angel-cake rules for beating egg whites and folding in sugar and flour hold true with sponge cakes, too. Another important rule to follow is to beat egg yolks till they're lemon-colored and thick as whipped cream.

You may beat some or all of the sugar with the yolks, but remember to add sugar gradually. In some recipes, liquid is added to the yolks and then the mixture is beaten till it is very light and foamy.

Causes for failures with Angel and Sponge cakes

Tough cake
Too hot an oven
Not enough sugar
Overmixing

Cracks in crust
Overbeaten whites
Too much sugar
Too hot an oven

Coarse texture
Underbeaten whites
Insufficient blending of ingredients
Too slow an oven

Heavy sticky layer at bottom
Underbeaten egg yolks
Insufficient mixing of egg yolks with
    other ingredients

Sticky crust
Too much sugar
Underbaking

Undersize cake
Underbeaten or overbeaten whites
Overmixing
Too large a pan
Too hot an oven
Removing from pan too soon

Angel cake

1 c. sifted cake flour
¾ c. sugar
1½ c. (12) egg whites
1½ t. cream of tartar
¼ t. salt
1½ t. vanilla
¾ c. sugar

Preheat oven to 375° F.

Sift flour with ¾ cup sugar 4 times. Beat egg whites with cream of tartar, salt, and vanilla till stiff enough to form peaks but still moist and glossy. Add the remaining ¾ cup sugar, 2 tablespoons at a time, continuing to beat until meringue holds stiff peaks.

Sift about ¼ of flour mixture over whites; fold in. Fold in remaining flour by fourths. Bake in *ungreased* 10-in. tube pan in 375° F. oven for 35 to 40 min. or until tests done. Invert pan and let cake cool.

Variation. For chocolate angel cake, substitute ¾ cup sifted cake flour and ¼ cup cocoa for 1 cup sifted cake flour. Sift cocoa with flour and sugar 4 times.

Sponge cake

1⅓ c. flour, unsifted
½ t. baking powder
½ t. salt
1 c. sugar
1 t. cream of tartar
6 egg whites
½ c. sugar
6 egg yolks
¼ c. water
2 t. lemon extract

Preheat oven to 375° F.

Mix flour, baking powder, salt, and 1 cup sugar thoroughly. Add cream of tartar to egg whites; beat until soft peaks form. Add ½ cup sugar, a little at a time, and beat until stiff peaks form. Mix egg yolks, water, and lemon extract in a bowl. Stir flour mixture into egg yolk mixture. Beat well. Fold beaten egg whites into egg yolk/flour mixture, using about 40 strokes. Pour batter into an ungreased 10-in. tube pan (angel food tin). Bake 45 to 50 min. or until lightly browned. Invert pan to cool cake. Remove from pan when cool.

Variation. This recipe can be used for an easy-to-make and delicious sponge cake roll by preparing one half of the recipe: Line a 15x10x1-in. pan with wax paper or brown paper; grease. Spread batter evenly in pan. Bake 12 to 15 min. at 375° F. until center is firm when touched lightly. Place a sheet of wax paper on a rack. Sprinkle with ¼ cup confectioner's sugar. Turn cake onto paper. Peel top paper from cake and trim away any crusty edges of cake. Cool on rack. Spread with filling as desired. Jelly, whipped topping, or prepared pie filling may be used. Starting from narrow side, roll cake. Place seam side down. Sift confectioner's sugar over roll just before cutting and serving. Any favorite jelly or jam may be used as filling or a flavored whipped dessert topping or sweetened, flavored whipped cream alone with fresh blueberries or sliced, sweetened strawberries (well drained). Try a chilled roll using slightly softened ice cream. Place this in freezer until used.

Makes 12 servings.

Orange sponge cake

6 eggs, separated
½ c. orange juice
1 T. grated orange peel
1 c. sugar
¼ t. salt
1⅓ c. cake flour, sifted
1 t. cream of tartar
½ c. sugar

Preheat oven to 325° F.

Beat egg yolks until thick and lemon-colored. Add orange peel and orange juice; beat until very thick. Gradually beat in 1 cup sugar and the salt. Fold in flour, a little at a time. Beat egg whites with the cream of tartar until soft peaks form. Gradually add ½ cup sugar, beating until stiff peaks form. Thoroughly fold whites into yolk mixture. Bake in ungreased 10-in. tube pan about 55 min., or until done. Invert pan to cool. Spoon on orange glaze (1½ cups sifted confectioners' sugar mixed with 2 tablespoons orange juice); trim with orange sections.

Makes one 10-in. cake.

Butter sponge

1 c. sifted cake flour
1 t. baking powder
¼ c. butter, melted
½ t. vanilla
½ c. milk, scalded
6 egg yolks
1 c. sugar

Preheat oven to 350° F.
Grease a 9x9x2-in. pan.

Sift together flour and baking powder. Scald the milk. Add butter and vanilla to milk and keep hot. Beat egg yolks until thick and lemon-colored; gradually beat in sugar. Quickly add flour mixture; stir just until mixed. Gently stir in the hot milk mixture.

Bake 30 to 35 min. or until done. Cool thoroughly. Do not invert pan.

Makes one 9-in. cake.

Sponge cake roll

6 eggs, separated
½ t. cream of tartar
¼ t. salt
1 c. confectioners' sugar
1 t. vanilla
¾ c. all-purpose flour

Preheat oven to 400° F.
Lightly grease a
   15½x10½x1-in. jelly
   roll pan.
Line bottom with waxed
   paper and grease
   again.

In mixing bowl, beat at high speed the egg whites, cream of tartar, and salt until stiff but not dry, just until whites no longer slip when bowl is tilted. In large bowl, beat egg yolks at high speed until thick and lemon-colored, about 5 min. Gradually beat in confectioners' sugar and vanilla. Gently but thoroughly fold flour and whites into yolk mixture. Pour into prepared pan, spreading evenly. Bake until top of cake springs back when touched lightly with finger, 10 to 12 min. Cover a clean towel with waxed paper. Sprinkle paper lightly with confectioners' sugar. Loosen cake from sides of pan with spatula and invert onto prepared towel. Carefully pull waxed paper off bottom of cake and discard. Trim all edges. Starting from narrow edge, roll up cake, rolling sugared waxed paper in with cake. Wrap in towel and place seam-side-down on wire rack until cool, about 30 min.

To prepare cake roll, carefully unroll cake and spread with whipped cream, jelly, or other filling. Reroll. Place on serving plate and chill. Just before serving, dust with confectioners' sugar, if desired.

Variation. For chocolate sponge roll, combine ¼ cup cocoa with 1 cup confectioners' sugar. Add to beaten egg yolks and proceed as directed in sponge cake recipe.

note: If prepared in advance, cake may be frozen without filling. Wrap well with aluminum foil or plastic wrap. To thaw, let wrapped cake stand at room temperature 1 hour.

Makes 8 to 10 servings.

Chocolate chiffon cake

2 eggs, separated
1½ c. sugar
1¾ c. sifted cake flour
¾ t. baking soda
½ t. salt
⅓ c. oil
1 c. buttermilk
2 squares unsweetened
  chocolate, melted
1 t. vanilla

*chocolate marshmallow
  icing*
8 marshmallows
⅓ c. milk
1 t. vanilla
2 c. confectioners' sugar
3 T. cocoa
dash salt

Preheat oven to 350° F.
Grease generously with
  butter and dust with
  flour two 8-in. layer
  cake pans.

Beat egg whites until frothy. Gradually beat in ½ cup of the sugar. Continue beating until very stiff and glossy. Set meringue aside. Sift remaining sugar, flour, baking soda, and salt into another bowl. Add oil and half of the buttermilk. Beat with mixer on medium speed for 1 min. Scrape sides and bottom of bowl constantly. Add remaining buttermilk, egg yolks, melted chocolate, and vanilla. Beat 1 more min., scraping bowl constantly. Fold in meringue. Pour into the layer cake pans. Bake 30 to 35 min. Frost with chocolate marshmallow icing.

Melt marshmallows slowly over low heat, adding milk gradually and blending in. Add remaining ingredients, beating continuously to maintain smooth consistency. Cool before spreading.

Makes one 8-in. layer cake.

Party chiffon cake

2 c. sifted all-purpose
  flour
1½ c. sugar
3 t. baking powder
1 t. salt
½ c. oil
7 eggs, separated
¾ c. cold water
2 t. vanilla
½ t. cream of tartar

Sift first 4 ingredients together in large mixing bowl. Mix well, add oil, egg yolks, water, and vanilla. Beat with electric beater at medium speed 1 min. until smooth. Add cream of tartar to egg whites and beat until whites form very stiff peaks. Pour egg yolk mixture gradually over beaten egg whites, gently folding with rubber scraper until just blended. Do not stir. Pour immediately into ungreased 10-in. tube pan. Bake for 55 min. then increase heat to 350° F. for 10 to 15 min., or until top springs back when lightly touched. Invert pan on rack until cool.

Preheat oven to 325° F.

Makes one 10-in. cake.

Angel cake divine

1 c. sifted cake flour
1¼ c. sifted
  confectioners' sugar
1½ c. egg whites (10–12
  eggs)
1½ t. cream of tartar
¼ t. salt
1½ t. vanilla
¼ t. almond extract
1 c. granulated sugar

Sift flour with confectioners' sugar 3 times. Beat egg whites with cream of tartar, salt, vanilla, and almond extract until stiff enough to stand in soft peaks, but still moist and glossy. Beat in the granulated sugar, 2 tablespoonfuls at a time, continue to beat until the meringue holds stiff peaks.

Sift about ¼ of flour mixture over egg white mixture; turn the bowl while folding the flour in lightly with a down-up-and-over motion. In the same way, fold in the remaining flour by fourths. Bake in an ungreased 10-in. tube pan about 30 min. or until done. Invert pan and cool cake thoroughly.

Preheat oven to 375° F.

Makes one 10-in. cake.

Chocolate angel food cake

¾ c. sifted cake flour
¼ c. cocoa
¼ t. salt
1¼ c. egg whites (10 to 12 eggs)
1 t. cream of tartar
1¼ c. sifted confectioners' sugar
1 t. vanilla

Sift flour and cocoa together 4 times. Add salt to egg whites; beat until frothy. Add cream of tartar. Beat until stiff enough to form peaks. Fold sugar into whites, ¼ cup at a time. Add vanilla. Fold flour mixture into whites, 2 tablespoonfuls at a time.

Pour batter into ungreased 10-in. angel food pan. Bake 1 hour. Invert pan on rack and let cake cool about 1 hour. After removing pan, brush off any loose cake crumbs so frosting will go on smoothly. Frost with orange frosting.

orange frosting
1 pkg. cream cheese (3-oz.)
1 T. orange juice
2½ c. sifted confectioners' sugar
½ t. grated orange rind

Blend cream cheese and orange juice. Add the sugar gradually, blending well. Add orange rind; blend again. Makes enough frosting for one 10-in. tube pan cake.

Makes one 10-in. cake.

Preheat oven to 375° F.

Apple cobbler

⅔ c. sugar
3 T. quick-cooking
  tapioca
⅛ t. salt
1½ c. water
5 c. apples, pared and
  sliced (about 5
  medium apples)
1 c. flour, unsifted
1½ t. baking powder
¼ t. salt
3 T. shortening
⅓ c. milk
  (approximately)
2 T. sugar
1 t. cinnamon

Mix sugar, tapioca, ⅛ teaspoon salt, and water in a large saucepan. Let stand while preparing apples. Bring tapioca mixture to a full boil, stirring to prevent sticking. Add apples. Boil gently, covered, until apples are tender, 5 to 10 min. Stir occasionally to prevent sticking. Pour apple mixture into a 2-quart casserole. Mix flour, baking powder, and ¼ teaspoon salt thoroughly. Mix in shortening with a pastry blender or fork until mixture is crumbly. Stir in milk, using just enough to make a dough that is soft but not sticky. Press dough evenly onto apple mixture in casserole. Mix 2 tablespoons sugar with cinnamon; sprinkle onto dough. Bake for 20 to 25 min., or until nicely browned. Serve warm or cold with cream, whipped cream, or sour cream if desired.

Makes 6 servings.

Preheat oven to 400° F.

Peach cobbler

1½ T. cornstarch
¼ c. brown sugar, firmly
  packed
½ c. water
4 c. peeled, sliced fresh
  peaches
1 T. butter
1 T. lemon juice
1 T. sugar
⅓ c. sour cream
1 T. milk
1 c. buttermilk biscuit
  mix
1 T. sugar
⅛ t. nutmeg
cream, whipped cream,
  or sour cream
  (optional)

Preheat oven to 400° F.
Butter a 1-quart baking
  dish.

Mix cornstarch, brown sugar, and water together in a saucepan. Cook, stirring, until the mixture is thickened. Add the peach slices and heat a few min. longer. Remove the saucepan from the heat, and stir in the butter and lemon juice. Pour the mixture into the prepared baking dish.

Combine the 1 tablespoon sugar, sour cream, milk, and buttermilk biscuit mix; spoon over the hot peaches.

Combine 1 tablespoon sugar with the nutmeg, and sprinkle over the top. Bake for 20 to 25 min., or until nicely browned. Serve warm or cold with cream, whipped cream, or sour cream, if desired.

Makes 6 servings.

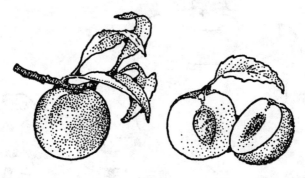

Pineapple carrot cake

2 c. flour
2 t. baking soda
1¼ t. salt
2 t. cinnamon
4 eggs
2 c. sugar
1 c. oil or melted butter
2 c. grated carrots
2 c. crushed pineapple
  (drained)
1 c. walnuts or fresh
  coconut

Sift together dry ingredients; set aside. Mix eggs, sugar, and oil; stir well. Add carrots, pineapple, and nuts or coconut, beating after each addition. Add sifted ingredients and mix well. Pour into the prepared baking pan and bake for 40 min. Frost with whipped cream icing or cream cheese icing.

Makes one 9x13-in. cake.

Preheat oven to 350° F.
Grease and flour a 9x13-
  in. pan.

Apple crisp

4 to 6 tart cooking
  apples
⅓ c. flour
1 c. uncooked quick
  rolled oats
½ c. brown sugar,
  packed
½ t. salt
1 t. cinnamon
⅓ c. melted margarine
  or butter

Pare and slice apples. Put them in the prepared pan. Stir dry ingredients together. Mix in shortening until the mixture is crumbly. Sprinkle topping over apples. Bake about 30 min. until apples are tender and topping is lightly browned.

Makes 6 servings.

Preheat oven to 375° F.
Grease a baking pan.

Cakes, tortes, and frostings

Pineapple upside-down cake

½ c. butter or
   margarine
2 c. brown sugar, firmly
   packed
1 large can sliced
   pineapple, drained
walnuts
maraschino cherries

Melt butter or margarine in 9-in. skillet (2-in. deep). Cover skillet bottom with brown sugar, spreading it evenly. Place 1 whole slice of pineapple in center on top of sugar. Cut remaining slices in half and arrange them in a circle around the center slice like the spokes of a wheel, rounded edges facing one way. Fill spaces in between with walnuts and maraschino cherries.

cake batter
4 eggs
1 c. sugar
1 c. cake flour
1 t. baking powder

Beat eggs well with mixer at high speed. Add sugar and continue to beat. Add flour sifted with baking powder. Pour batter over pineapple arrangement in skillet and bake 40 to 55 min., or until firm. Turn out upside-down on cake plate.

Makes one 9-in. cake.

Preheat oven to 350° F.

Apple pudding cake

4 apples (or more)
1 c. sugar
pinch of salt
1 c. flour
1 t. baking powder
1 egg
2 T. sugar (for top)
nutmeg
cinnamon
2 T. butter

Slice apples thinly and place in the pan. Sift together 1 cup sugar, salt, flour, and baking powder. Beat the egg and add to the dry ingredients. Spread this mixture on top of apples. Sprinkle 2 tablespoons sugar, mixed with the cinnamon and nutmeg on top. Dot with butter. Sprinkle with ¼ cup cold water. Bake for 45 min.

Makes one 8-in. cake

Preheat oven to 350° F.
Grease an 8x8-in pan.

Blueberry upside-down cake

1 pt. blueberries
¾ c. sugar
¼ c. shortening
1 egg
1 c. flour
1½ c. flour
1½ t. baking powder
⅛ t. salt
½ c. milk

Pour berries into the casserole. Sprinkle with ¼ cup of the sugar. Cream shortening, ½ cup sugar, and egg. Sift flour, baking powder, and salt. Add dry ingredients to the creamed mixture alternately with milk. Pour batter on top of the blueberries. Bake for 45 min. Serve cold or warm with ice cream or vanilla sauce.

Makes 6 servings.

Preheat oven to 375° F.
Butter a 1½-quart
   casserole.

Pumpkin cake

4 eggs
2 c. sugar
1½ c. oil
2 c. canned pumpkin
3 c. sifted flour
2 t. cinnamon
3 t. baking powder
2 t. baking soda
1 t. salt
1 c. raisins
1 c. chopped nuts

Beat eggs. Add sugar and beat until creamy. Sift together the dry ingredients. Add oil and pumpkin to the creamed mixture; mix well. Add the dry ingredients next, then the raisins and nuts. Mix well after each addition. Bake in prepared pan for 1¼ to 1½ hours. Cake may be iced with orange glaze.

Makes 8 to 10 servings.

Preheat oven to 350° F.
Grease well a bundt pan.

Carrot cake

cake
2 c. sugar
1½ c. vegetable oil
4 eggs, beaten
1 t. vanilla
2 c. flour
2 t. baking powder
2 t. baking soda
2 t. cinnamon
1 c. chopped walnuts
3 c. finely-grated carrots

Beat together sugar and oil. Add well-beaten eggs and vanilla; mix well. Sift together flour, baking powder, baking soda, and cinnamon. Gradually add dry ingredients to the creamed mixture. Carefully fold in walnuts and grated carrots. Bake for 40 min. in a 9x12-in. pan or 50 min. in a bundt pan.

frosting
6-oz. cream cheese, softened
⅓ c. butter or margarine
1½ t. vanilla
2 c. confectioners' sugar

For the frosting, cream together softened cream cheese and butter. Add confectioners' sugar and mix well. Add the vanilla. Spread on cooled cake.

Makes 8 to 10 servings.

Preheat oven to 350° F.

Black bottom cupcakes

cream cheese mixture

8-oz. softened cream
    cheese
1 egg
½ c. sugar
⅛ t. salt
6-oz. semi-sweet
    chocolate bits

For cream cheese mixture, combine first 4 ingredients and mix well. Stir in chocolate bits.

cocoa batter

1½ c. flour
1 c. sugar
¼ c. cocoa
½ t. salt
1 c. water
⅓ c. cooking oil
1 T. vinegar
1 t. vanilla

For cocoa batter, sift first four ingredients. Add water, oil, vinegar, and vanilla. Beat vigorously. Fill each muffin cup ⅓ full of cocoa batter. Top each with 1 heaping tablespoonful cream cheese mixture. Bake for 30 to 35 min. The cupcakes may be served after cooking or can be frozen for later use. Just defrost to serve.

Makes about 2 dozen cupcakes.

Preheat oven to 350° F.
Line miniature muffin
    tins with paper
    baking cups.

Nancy's cupcakes

⅓ c. shortening
2 c. sifted cake flour
1 c. sugar
2½ t. baking powder
¾ t. salt
¾ c. milk
1 slightly beaten egg
1 t. vanilla

Stir shortening to soften. Stir in dry ingredients. Add half the milk and the egg. Mix until flour is dampened. Beat 2 min. at low speed with an electric mixer. Add remaining milk and vanilla; beat 1 min. longer. Fill each muffin cup ½ full. Bake about 20 min. or until done.

Makes 20 cupcakes.

Preheat oven to 375° F.
Line muffin tins with
   paper baking cups.

Fudgy cupcakes

⅔ c. brown sugar
⅓ c. milk
2 (1-oz.) squares
   unsweetened
   chocolate
⅓ c. shortening
⅔ c. brown sugar or
   granulated sugar
1 t. vanilla
2 eggs
1⅓ c. sifted all-purpose
   flour
1 t. soda
½ t. salt
½ c. milk

Combine ⅔ cup brown sugar, ⅓ cup milk, and chocolate in saucepan; heat and stir over very low heat until chocolate melts; cool. Stir shortening to soften. Gradually add ⅔ cup brown or granulated sugar; cream together until light and fluffy. Add vanilla. Add eggs, one at a time, beating well after each addition.
   Sift flour with soda and salt; add to creamed mixture alternately with ½ cup milk, a little at a time. Beat after each addition. Add chocolate mixture and beat well. Fill each muffin cup ½ full. Bake about 20 min., or until done.

Makes about 2 dozen cupcakes.

Preheat oven to 375° F.
Line muffin tins with
   paper baking cups.

Chocolate cupcakes

2 (1-oz.) squares baking
   chocolate
1 c. strong coffee
¾ c. butter or
   margarine
1 c. sugar
2 eggs
1¾ c. sifted cake flour
1 t. baking soda
1 t. vanilla
chocolate mint chips
chopped nuts
confectioners' sugar

Melt chocolate and combine with coffee. Cream butter and sugar, add eggs and mix well. Sift flour with baking soda and add to butter mixture alternately with the chocolate mixture. Add vanilla and mix well. Pour batter into muffin cups so that each cup is ¾ full. Top each cupcake with several chocolate chips and nuts. Bake 20 min. Remove from oven and sprinkle with sifted confectioners' sugar.

Makes about 2 dozen cupcakes.

Preheat oven to 325° F.
Line muffin tins with
   paper baking cups.

Peanut butter cupcakes

½ c. peanut butter
⅓ c. shortening
1 t. vanilla
1½ c. brown sugar
2 eggs
2 c. sifted all-purpose
   flour
2 t. baking powder
½ t. salt
¾ c. milk

Cream together peanut butter, shortening, and vanilla. Gradually add brown sugar, beating until light and fluffy. Add eggs, one at a time, beating well after each addition.

Sift together dry ingredients; add alternately with milk to creamed mixture. Fill muffin cups ½ full. Bake 20 min. or until done. Frost each cupcake with peanut butter and sift confectioners' sugar on top.

Makes about 2 dozen cupcakes.

Preheat oven to 375° F.
Line muffin tins with
   paper baking cups.

Easy pound cake

1½ c. sugar
1 c. butter
4 eggs
¼ t. salt
dash nutmeg
2 c. cake flour
½ c. milk

Put all ingredients in a bowl and beat 10 min. Pour into tube pan; bake 1 hour.

Makes 1 loaf.

Preheat oven to 350° F.
Grease a tube pan.

Devil's food cake with fudge frosting

cake
4-oz. baking chocolate, chopped
½ c. milk
¾ c. turbinado sugar
1 egg yolk, slightly beaten
2 c. sifted cake flour
1 t. baking powder
1 t. baking soda
½ t. salt
½ c. butter
¾ c. sugar
2 egg yolks
¾ c. milk
2 t. vanilla extract
2 egg whites

To make the cake, combine baking chocolate, ½ cup milk, and ¾ cup sugar in the top of a double boiler. Add the egg yolk. Place the pot over hot water and cook, stirring, until the chocolate melts and the mixture thickens. Remove from heat and set aside.

Sift together the cake flour, baking powder, baking soda, and salt. Cream the butter and gradually add ¾ cup sugar. Add 2 egg yolks, one at a time, beating well after each addition. Add the flour mixture alternately with ¾ cup milk combined with the vanilla extract. Add the chocolate mixture and blend well. Beat the egg whites until stiff and fold them into the batter. Turn the mixture into the cake pan and bake for about 30 min., or until a cake tester inserted in the center comes out clean. Cool on a wire rack.

frosting
1 c. milk
2 c. sugar
2-oz. baking chocolate, chopped
pinch of salt
3 T. butter
1 t. vanilla extract

Preheat oven to 350° F.
Butter and flour a 9x12-in. cake pan.

To make the frosting, combine the milk, sugar, chopped baking chocolate, and salt in a heavy saucepan. Cook over medium heat, stirring, until the chocolate has melted. Bring the mixture ot a boil, lower the heat, and cook without stirring, partially covered, to the soft-ball stage, about 238° F. Remove the pan from the heat and place in a bowl of ice cubes or shaved ice. Stir the frosting until the temperature drops to about 130° F. Add the butter and stir until it has melted. Add the vanilla extract. Beat until the frosting begins to stiffen and is of the proper consistency to spread. Ice the cake immediately.

Makes about 15 servings.

Chocolate chip cake

1 c. sugar
2 eggs
¼ lb. butter
½ pt. sour cream
2 c. sifted flour
1½ t. baking powder
1 t. baking soda
1 t. vanilla
½ c. chocolate chips

topping
½ c. sugar
2 t. cinnamon
½ c. walnuts
2 heaping t. cocoa (not
    cocoa mix)

Preheat oven to 350° F.
Grease and flour a 9 or
    10-in. tube pan.

Mix together the topping ingredients; set aside. Mix and beat first three ingredients. Sift together flour, baking powder, and soda. Add the dry ingredients with sour cream and vanilla to the creamed mixture. Spread half the batter in pan, and sprinkle with half of the topping. Pour on the remaining batter and add the rest of the topping. Sprinkle the chocolate chips on top. Marbelize by running knife through batter. Bake for 40 to 50 min.

Makes one 9 or 10-in. cake.

Note: This is a good coffee cake if chocolate chips and cocoa are left out.

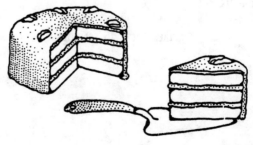

THE DESSERT COOKBOOK

Chocolate mocha layer cake

1½ square unsweetened chocolate (1½-oz.) or 6 T. unsweetened cocoa powder
4 T. butter
1⅛ c. cake flour
2 t. baking powder
dash of salt
1 c. sugar
2 eggs
½ c. milk
1 t. vanilla

In top of double boiler, melt chocolate and butter. Sift together flour, baking powder, salt, and sugar. Break eggs into mixture, stir, and add milk. Stir well; add butter and chocolate. Stir in vanilla. Pour into the prepared cake pans. Bake for 15 to 20 min. or until knife comes out clean. Remove from pans and place cakes on racks. Frost when cool.

mocha frosting
2 c. confectioners' sugar
1 square unsweetened chocolate (1 oz.)
4 T. butter, melted
1 t. vanilla
½ c. strong black coffee

Melt butter and chocolate, remove from fire and add sugar and vanilla. Moisten with warm coffee until the frosting can be spread. Dip the knife into the coffee while frosting the cake.

Makes one 8-in. layer cake.

Preheat oven to 350° F.
Grease two 8-in. cake pans.

Mississippi mud cake

3 squares semi-sweet
  chocolate (3-oz.)
1½ c. boiling water
¼ lb. margarine
2 c. sugar
1 t. salt
1 t. baking soda
2 eggs, slightly beaten
2 c. flour

Melt chocolate in boiling water. Cool to room temperature. Add rest of ingredients; mix well. Bake in tube pan for 1¼ hours. This is a moist cake that doesn't need icing.

Makes 1 long cake.

Preheat oven to 275° F.

Hazelnut cream cake

1 c. heavy cream
2 eggs
1 t. vanilla extract
1½ c. flour
¾ c. sugar
2 t. baking powder
pinch of salt
3 T. butter
⅓ c. free-flowing brown
  sugar
½ c. chopped hazelnuts
1 T. flour

Reserve 1 tablespoon of heavy cream and whip the rest until stiff. Beat in the eggs, 1 at a time, mixing well each time. Add the vanilla extract. Sift the 1½ cups flour, the sugar, baking powder, and salt together twice, and stir into batter. Pour into the spring-form pan and bake for 35 min., or until a cake tester inserted in the center comes out clean.

While the cake is baking, combine the butter, brown sugar, hazelnuts, 1 tablespoon flour, and the reserved 1 tablespoon heavy cream in a small saucepan. Heat until the butter has melted and all ingredients are blended.

When the cake has baked for 35 min., spread the topping over the cake and return to oven for 10 min. Cool on a cake rack; remove the sides of the pan when cool.

Preheat oven to 350° F.
Butter and flour a 9-in.
  spring-form pan.

Makes 8 servings.

Applesauce cake

1⅓ c. plus 2 T. flour
1 t. baking soda
½ t. salt
½ t. cinnamon
¼ t. ground cloves
¼ t. allspice
¼ c. soft shortening
1 c. sugar
1 egg
1 c. applesauce
¼ c. pecans or walnuts
½ c. raisins

Sift together 1⅓ cup flour, baking soda, cinnamon, cloves, allspice, and salt. Beat shortening, sugar, and egg in mixing bowl until light and fluffy. Add dry ingredients alternately with applesauce to the creamed mixture, beginning and ending with dry ingredients. Scrape bowl frequently during mixing. Mix nuts, raisins, and remaining flour together. Fold into batter. Pour into the prepared pan, and bake for 40 to 45 min. Cool in pan for 10 min. Frost, if desired, with orange butter-cream icing.

*orange butter-cream
  icing*
½ c. butter
½ t. vanilla
1 c. sifted confectioners'
  sugar
1 t. grated orange rind
2 T. orange juice

Blend butter, vanilla, and sugar thoroughly. Beat in orange rind and orange juice. Beat until icing can be easily spread. If too stiff, a little more orange juice may be used. Spread on top of cake.

Makes one 9-in. cake.

Preheat oven to 350° F.
Grease a 9x9-in. pan.

Sour cream coffee cake

½ c. margarine
1 c. sugar
2 eggs
2 c. sifted all-purpose
  flour
1 t. baking soda
1 t. baking powder
½ t. salt
1 c. sour cream
1 t. vanilla

Cream margarine; add sugar. Beat until light and fluffy. Add eggs, one at a time, beating well after each addition. Sift dry ingredients together and add alternately with sour cream to egg mixture. Add vanilla. Pour half the batter into a well-greased 9-in. tube pan, or a well-greased 9x13-in. pan. Cover with nut mixture. Pour remaining batter over top of nut mixture. Bake 40 min.

Makes one 9x13-in. cake.

nut mixture
½ c. dark brown sugar
2 T. flour
½ t. cinnamon
2 T. margarine
½ c. chopped nuts

Preheat oven to 325° F.

Orange cake

2 sponge cake layers
½ c. sugar
1 T. cornstarch
2 egg yolks, slightly
  beaten
1 c. orange juice
juice of 1 lemon
rind of 1 orange
3 egg whites
heavy cream, whipped

In a saucepan, combine sugar, cornstarch, and egg yolks; heat. Add orange juice, lemon juice, and orange rind; cook until creamy. Beat egg whites and fold into mixture. Fill between the layers of the cake with the frosting. Ice the top of the cake. Chill at least 12 hours. Before serving, cover with whipped cream.

Makes 8 to 10 servings.

Cinnamon sour cream cake

½ c. butter
2 c. sugar
4 eggs
2 c. sour cream
2 t. baking soda
2½ c. flour
3 t. baking powder
2 t. vanilla

topping
½ c. sugar
2 t. cinnamon
1 c. chopped pecans
   (optional)

Mix topping ingredients together; set aside. Cream together butter and 2 cups sugar. Beat together eggs, sour cream, and baking soda; add to butter mixture. Sift together flour and baking powder; add vanilla and blend with first mixture.

   Spread half the batter in a 9x13-in. pan. Sprinkle half of the topping on the batter. Add rest of batter and sprinkle with remainder of topping. Bake 35 to 45 min.

Makes one 9x13-in. cake.

Preheat oven to 350° F.

Lemon cake

1 pkg. yellow cake mix
4 eggs
¾ c. vegetable oil
¾ c. apricot nectar
1 pkg. lemon gelatin
   (3-oz.)
2 T. lemon flavoring
1½ c. confectioners'
   sugar
juice of 2 lemons

Mix cake mix, egg yolks, oil, apricot nectar, gelatin, and lemon flavoring. Stiffly beat the egg whites and fold them into the batter. Pour the mixture into an ungreased 9-in. tube pan. Bake for 1 hour or until toothpick inserted in cake comes out clean. In a pot, mix confectioners' sugar and lemon juice (can also add a little apricot nectar). Put the pot on top of stove (not on a burner) to warm while cake is cooking. When cake is done, let it stand in the pan, right-side-up, for 10 min. Remove from pan, prick with a fork all over, then spread with lemon mixture.

Preheat oven to 325° F.   Makes 8 to 10 servings.

Lemon buttermilk cake

1 stick butter
½ c. shortening
2 c. sugar
3 eggs
3 c. flour
½ t. soda
½ t. salt
1 c. buttermilk
1 t. vanilla
2 t. lemon juice
2 t. grated lemon rind
1 stick soft butter
2 c. confectioners' sugar
juice of 2 lemons

Cream together 1 stick butter, shortening, and 2 cups sugar. Add eggs, one at a time, mixing after each addition. Sift together flour, soda, and salt. Add these dry ingredients to the buttermilk, vanilla, 2 teaspoons lemon juice, and grated lemon rind. Bake for 1 hour in bundt pan or tube pan.

Mix together the soft butter, confectioners' sugar, and lemon juice. Glaze the cake while hot with this mixture.

Makes 8 to 10 servings.

Preheat oven to 350° F.

Mandarin orange cake

2 eggs
1 can (11.5-oz.)
   mandarin oranges,
   undrained
2 c. sugar
2 c. flour
2 t. baking soda
½ t. salt
¼ c. brown sugar
3 T. milk
2 T. butter

Beat eggs; add the oranges. Sift together sugar, flour, baking soda, and salt; add to the first mixture. Beat for 4 min. Pour into pan. Bake for 30 to 35 min. (If oranges are too juicy, the cake will take longer to cook. Test with toothpick, which should come out clean. In the meantime, bring to a boil the brown sugar, milk, and butter. Pour over hot cake as soon as it comes from the oven.

Makes 6 servings.

Preheat oven to 350° F.
Grease and flour
   9x13x2-in. pan.

THE DESSERT COOKBOOK

Fruit cocktail cake

2 eggs
1 can fruit cocktail,
    undrained
1½ c. sugar
2 c. flour
½ t. salt
2 t. soda
1 t. vanilla
½ c. brown sugar
1½ c. flaky coconut

Mix together eggs and fruit cocktail. Add sugar and mix well. Sift together flour, salt, and soda; add the egg mixture to the dry ingredients. Add vanilla. Mix well. Put into pan; sprinkle with brown sugar and coconut. Bake for 30 min., or until done.

Makes 6 servings.

Preheat oven to 350° F.
Grease and flour
    9x13x2-in. pan.

Pistachio cake

1 square (1-oz.)
    chocolate melted
4 eggs
½ c. salad oil
1 c. orange juice
1 pkg. instant pistachio
    pudding
1 pkg. instant cake mix

Beat eggs and add oil. Stir in juice. Mix cake mix and pudding together and add to egg mixture. Pour into the prepared pan ¾ of the batter. Melt the chocolate and add it to the remaining batter; pour over the other batter. Bake for 1 hour. Let the cake cool in pan for 15 min. or more and continue to cool on a rack. Sprinkle with confectioners' sugar. Serve with pistachio ice cream.

Makes one 10-in. cake.

Preheat oven to 350° F.
Grease a 10-in. angel
    food pan.

Kentucky butter cake

3 c. flour
1 t. baking powder
1 t. salt
½ t. baking soda
1 c. butter
2 c. sugar
4 eggs
1 c. buttermilk
2 t. vanilla

topping
1 c. sugar
¼ c. water
½ c. butter
1 T. vanilla

Sift first four ingredients. Cream butter and sugar. Add eggs, one at a time, to the creamed mixture, beat well. Add buttermilk and vanilla. Combine this mixture with dry ingredients. Pour the batter into a 10-in. tube pan; bake for 60 to 65 min.

While the cake is baking, make the topping. Dissolve the sugar in the water; add the butter and vanilla. Heat until the mixture is a creamy syrup.

When the cake is done, leave it in the pan and prick holes in it with a fork. Loosen the edges. Pour the topping over the cake. Allow mixture to sink into and around cake. Turn out, and sprinkle with confectioners' sugar. Rum or brandy extract may be added to topping, if desired.

Makes one 10-in. cake.

Preheat oven to 325° F.

Cockeyed cake

1½ c. flour
1 c. sugar
1 t. soda
½ t. salt
3 T. cocoa
5 T. salad oil
1 T. vinegar
1 t. vanilla
1 c. cold water

Sift together flour, sugar, soda, salt, and cocoa into the prepared pan. Make three holes in the dry mixture. Pour oil into one hole, vinegar in the next, vanilla in the last. Pour cold water over all. Beat with spoon until smooth. Bake for 30 min.

Note: Batter may be mixed in bowl and poured into baking pan.

Makes 6 to 8 servings.

Preheat oven to 350° F.
Grease a 9x9x2-in. pan.

THE DESSERT COOKBOOK

Lazy daisy cake

2 eggs
1 c. sugar
1 t. vanilla
1 c. flour
1 t. baking powder
½ t. salt
½ c. milk
1 T. butter

Beat eggs until thick and lemon-colored. Add sugar gradually and continue beating. Add vanilla. Sift together flour, baking powder, and salt. Add this to first mixture and stir. Heat milk and butter just to the boiling point and add to mixture. Pour into buttered cake pan and bake for 45 min. (Put cake in oven *immediately* after adding hot milk.)

icing
3 T. butter
2 T. cream
3 T. brown sugar
1 c. coconut
1 t. vanilla

Warm first 3 ingredients together in saucepan. Add coconut and vanilla. Spread this on warm cake and place under broiler. Brown the top but watch it closely to prevent burning.

Makes 6 to 8 servings.

Preheat oven to 325° F.
Butter cake pan.

Gingerbread

½ c. butter
½ c. sugar
1 egg, beaten
1 c. molasses
2½ c. sifted all-purpose
   flour
1½ t. soda
½ t. salt
½ t. cloves
1 t. cinnamon
1 t. ginger
1 c. hot water

lemon sauce
1 c. sugar
2 T. cornstarch
2 c. boiling water
juice and grated rind of
   1 lemon
2 T. butter
¼ t. salt

Preheat oven to 350° F.
Grease a 9x13x2½-in.
   pan.

Cream butter well. Gradually add sugar and beat until light and fluffy. Add beaten egg and molasses. Add the dry ingredients which have been sifted together. Add the hot water last and beat until smooth. Pour into the prepared pan and bake 45 min. Cut in squares. Serve plain or decorate with whipped cream and cherry on top, or serve warm with lemon sauce.

Makes one 9x13-in. cake.

Mix sugar and cornstarch. Gradually add water. Cook over moderate heat, stirring constantly, until thick and clear. Add juice and rind of lemon, the butter, and salt. Serve hot over the gingerbread.

Makes one 9x13-in. cake.

Spice cake

3 eggs, separated
1 c. sugar
3 T. cold water
1 t. vanilla extract
1 t. lemon extract
1 t. almond extract
1½ T. cornstarch
1½ t. cinnamon
1 t. cocoa
⅛ t. ground cloves
all purpose flour
1½ t. baking powder
raspberry jam
confectioners' sugar

Beat egg yolks until light and lemon-colored. Add sugar and continue to beat until fluffy. Combine water and flavorings and add slowly to mixture. Place cornstarch, cinnamon, cocoa, and cloves in an 8-ounce measuring cup and fill remaining space in cup with sifted flour. Add these dry ingredients and the baking powder to the batter. Fold in stiffly beaten egg whites. Bake in prepared pan about 30 min. Split in half and spread with raspberry jam. Put together again. Sift confectioners' sugar over the top.

Makes one 8-in. cake.

Preheat oven to 350° F.
Grease well an 8-in.
  square pan or an
  8-in. tube pan.

Jelly roll

4 eggs, separated
¾ c. sugar
1 t. vanilla extract
¾ c. sifted cake flour
¾ t. baking powder
pinch of salt
sifted confectioners'
   sugar
¾ c. currant jelly

Preheat oven to 375° F.
Butter an 11x13x½-in.
   jelly roll pan, line it
   with waxed paper,
   and butter the waxed
   paper.

Beat the egg yolks, gradually add ½ cup of the sugar, and beat well. Add the vanilla extract. Sift together the cake flour, baking powder, and salt; gradually add to the egg yolk mixture. Beat the egg whites until soft peaks form. Add the remaining ¼ cup sugar gradually, and beat until the mixture is shiny. Fold into the batter, half at a time, folding gently but thoroughly until well blended. Turn the batter into the prepared pan, and spread it evenly with a rubber spatula. Bake for 10 to 13 min. until the cake is lightly browned and springs back when touched gently.

Remove the cake from the oven. With a sharp knife quickly trim off the outside edges. Sprinkle a dish towel with confectioners' sugar. Turn the cake right-side-down on the dish towel. Peel off the waxed paper. Roll up the cake with the towel, and set it on a wire rack to cool. When it is cool, unroll the cake and spread it thinly with currant jelly. Roll it up again and place it seam-side-down on a serving plate or board.

Variation. For lemon jelly roll, spread the cake with lemon curd instead of currant jelly.

Makes 8 servings.

Blueberry roll

2 c. flour
½ t. salt
1 T. baking powder
3 T. butter
¾ c. milk
T. melted butter
2 c. fresh blueberries
2 T. corn syrup
1 t. crystallized ginger,
 finely chopped
1 c. heavy cream
2 T. sugar or, preferably,
 1 T. syrup from jar of
 preserved ginger in
 syrup

Sift flour, salt, and baking powder into bowl and cut in butter with pastry blender or two knives. Quickly stir in the milk; knead gently for a moment, and turn dough out onto floured board. Roll out into a rectangle ⅛-in. thick. Brush with melted butter.

Wash and dry blueberries thoroughly and combine with the corn syrup and crystallized ginger. Spoon blueberry mixture over dough. Roll it up in jelly roll fashion. Brush edges with water and seal well. Brush top of pastry with milk. Place on prepared baking sheet and make 4 gashes on top to allow for escaping steam. Bake 25 min. Transfer to oval serving plate or long board.

Whip heavy cream just enough for it to hold its shape. Add sugar or ginger syrup. Transfer cream to serving bowl and serve with blueberry roll.

Preheat oven to 400° F.
Grease baking sheet.

Makes 10 to 12 servings.

Strawberry cheese roll

1 pkg. angel food cake
  mix
confectioners' sugar
2 pt. strawberries
1 pkg. cream cheese,
  softened (8-oz.)
3 T. milk
½ t. nutmeg

Preheat oven to 350° F.
Line a 15½x10¼x1-in.
  jelly roll pan with
  waxed paper.

Prepare angel food cake mix as label directs. Pour butter into jelly roll pan, spreading evenly. Bake 35 to 40 min. or until top springs back when lightly touched.

Dust a towel well with confectioners' sugar. Invert cake onto towel; carefully and quickly peel off waxed paper. Cut crisp edges from cake. Starting from narrow end, gently roll cake and towel together. Rest seam-side-down on rack to cool.

When cake is cool, thinly slice 1 pint strawberries. In small bowl, with electric mixer at medium speed, blend cream cheese, milk, and nutmeg until smooth. Gently unroll cake; spread with cream cheese mixture. Cover cream cheese with sliced strawberries; reroll cake and sprinkle generously with confectioners' sugar. Place on serving platter and refrigerate until ready to use. The remaining strawberries can be sliced or used whole. Sugar can be added to them, if desired. Pass the strawberries with slices of the roll.

Makes 8 to 10 servings.

Apple torte

4 c. cooking apples
1½ c. sugar
1 T. lemon juice
½ c. water
⅓ c. butter or
  margarine, melted
4-oz. currant jelly
4-oz. mixed ground nuts
1½ c. cake crumbs,
  toasted (pound cake
  is ideal)
12 macaroons
3-oz. sliced almonds,
  roasted
2 T. sugar
1 c. heavy cream

Core, peel, and slice apples as for a pie. Add 1½ cups sugar, lemon juice, and water. Cook in a large saucepan over moderate heat until tender. Drain.

Sprinkle ½ cup toasted cake crumbs over butter in souffle dish. Spread half the apple mixture on the crumbs. Top with the jelly, ground nuts, another ½ cup cake crumbs, and macaroons, in this order, spreading each evenly over the preceding layer. Add next the remaining apples, then the last ½ cup cake crumbs. Bake for 30 min. in the middle of the oven. When cooked, place in the refrigerator on a cooling rack for at least 2 hours.

Place the almonds on a baking sheet, lightly sprinkle with water, then 2 tablespoonfuls sugar, and roast at 350° F. for 15 to 20 min. or until golden. To serve, whip cream until stiff and spread evenly over the torte, then top with toasted almonds.

Preheat oven to 450° F.
Pour melted butter in
  the bottom of a 1½-2-
  quart souffle dish.

Makes 8 servings.

Easy apple torte

1 egg
¾ c. sugar
2 T. flour
1½ t. baking powder
⅛ t. salt
½ c. chopped nuts
½ c. chopped apples
1 t. vanilla

Beat egg and sugar until smooth. Mix flour, baking powder, and salt and add to egg mixture. Add nuts, apples, and vanilla. Bake for 35 min. Serve with whipped cream or ice cream.

Makes 6 servings.

Preheat oven to 350° F.
Grease a 9x9 1-in.
  casserole or a 9 or
  10-in. pie plate.

Swedish torte

batter
½ c. butter
½ c. sugar
4 egg yolks
¼ c. milk
2 t. baking powder
1 c. flour

Cream butter and sugar. Add egg yolks, one at a time, beating after each addition. Add flour and baking powder alternately with milk to the creamed mixture. Divide batter into two 9-in. round pans with removable bottoms.

meringue
4 egg whites
1 c. sugar
½ c. chopped nuts

To make meringue, beat egg whites and sugar until soft peaks form. Top each pan with meringue. Sprinkle chopped nuts on top. Bake 30 to 35 min. Let cool and remove from pans.

filling
½ c. whipped cream
1 pkg. frozen
   strawberries (10-oz.)
1 banana, sliced

Mix together the ½ cup whipped cream, drained frozen strawberries, and sliced banana. Fill between the layers with this mixture.

Makes 10 to 12 servings.

Preheat oven to 350° F.

Mocha whipped cream frosting

1½ pt. heavy whipping
   cream
5 t. instant coffee
   powder
2 T. instant cocoa
¼ c. unsifted
   confectioners' sugar
2 t. vanilla extract

Using an electric beater, beat cream at highest speed. When it begins to thicken slightly, very gradually add remaining ingredients, and beat until the frosting is thick enough to ice the cake. A portion of frosting may be reserved, placed in a canvas decorating bag and used to decorate the cake. The cake may also be decorated with shaved chocolate curls. Refrigerate for a few hours before serving.

Makes enough for 1 cake.

Mocha chocolate frosting

6 T. cocoa
6 T. hot coffee
6 T. butter
dash of salt
1 t. vanilla or rum
   extract
3 c. confectioners' sugar
chopped walnuts

Combine cocoa and hot coffee. Add butter, salt, and vanilla or rum extract, beating until smooth. Gradually add confectioners' sugar, beating until the frosting is of consistency to spread. After the cake is frosted, garnish with chopped walnuts.

Makes enough for 1 cake.

Seven-minute frosting

2 egg whites
1½ c. sugar
⅓ c. cold water
⅛ t. cream of tartar
⅛ t. salt
1 t. vanilla

In large saucepan, combine all ingredients except vanilla. Beat 1 minute at low speed with electric mixer. Place pan over low heat and beat at high speed until stiff peaks form, about 5 min. Remove from heat. Add vanilla. Beat until frosting will hold swirls, about 2 min. longer.

Makes 5 cups.

Cinnamon-coffee frosting

1 c. butter or margarine
1 t. cinnamon
few grains of salt
1 T. instant coffee
  powder
2 t. vanilla
6 c. sifted confectioners'
  sugar
½ c. milk (about)

Cream butter or margarine until consistency of mayonnaise. Blend in cinnamon, salt, coffee, and vanilla. Add sugar alternately with milk, beating constantly, until the icing is fluffy and easy to spread.

Makes enough to fill and frost a four layer 8 or 9-in. cake.

Caramel-nut frosting

½ c. butter or
  margarine
1 c. brown sugar, packed
¼ c. milk
2 c. confectioners' sugar
⅔ c. finely chopped
  pecans or walnuts
½ t. vanilla
nut halves, as desired

Combine shortening, brown sugar, and milk. Cook over medium heat, stirring constantly, only until mixture boils and sugar is dissolved. Cool slightly. Beat confectioners' sugar into cooked mixture until frosting reaches consistency to spread. Add chopped nuts and vanilla; mix well. Spread on cooled cake. Garnish with nut halves.

Makes enough for 1 cake.

Quick vanilla frosting

8-oz. cream cheese,
  softened
1 lb. confectioners'
  sugar, sifted
1 stick butter, softened
2 t. vanilla

Mix all the ingredients together. Add a little cream or milk if frosting is too thick for spreading.

Makes enough for 1 layer cake.

White icing

½ c. flour
½ c. milk
½ c. shortening
½ c. butter
½ c. granulated sugar

In a small bowl mix flour and milk. In a separate bowl, mix shortening butter, and sugar. Beat 2 min. Combine all ingredients and beat for 5 min., or until mixture is smooth and creamy. If a sweeter icing is desired, add more sugar.

Makes icing for one 9-in. layer cake or for a sheet cake.

Marshmallow icing

1 c. sugar
⅓ c. water
2 egg whites, stiffly beaten
⅓ t. cream of tartar
1½ t. vanilla

Boil sugar and water and add slowly to the stiffly beaten whites. While still warm, add cream of tartar and vanilla. Beat the ingredients until the bowl is cool.

Makes enough for one cake.

Chocolate marshmallow icing

5 (1-oz.) squares baking chocolate
5 T. butter
⅓ c. water
1 c. miniature marshmallows
4 c. sifted confectioners' sugar
1 c. ground nuts
2 t. vanilla

Melt chocolate combined with butter, water, and marshmallows over medium heat. Cool slightly. Add remaining ingredients and mix thoroughly. If icing is too thick, add a small amount of milk or cream.

Makes enough for three 9-in. layers.

Chocolate whipped cream frosting

¼ c. confectioners'
    sugar
2 T. cocoa
1½ c. whipping cream
½ t. vanilla

Sift together sugar and cocoa. Stir in heavy cream and vanilla. Chill at least 2 hours. When ready to use, whip to desired consistency.

Makes enough for one cake.

Fudge frosting

1 c. milk
2 c. sugar
2 (1-oz.) squares baking
    chocolate, chopped
pinch of salt
3 T. butter
1 t. vanilla extract

Combine milk, sugar, chopped chocolate, and salt in heavy saucepan. Cook over medium heat, stirring until chocolate has melted. Bring mixture to a boil, lower heat and cook without stirring, partially covered, to the soft-ball stage, about 238° F. Remove the pan from heat and place it in a bowl of ice cubes. Stir frosting until the temperature drops to about 130° F. Add the butter and stir until it has melted. Add the vanilla extract. Beat until the frosting begins to stiffen and is of the proper consistency to spread. Ice the cake immediately.

Makes enough for 1 cake.

Butter frosting

⅓ c. butter
4 c. confectioners' sugar
1 egg yolk
1½ t. vanilla
2 T. light cream
   (approximately)

Cream butter; gradually add about half the sugar, blending well. Beat in egg yolk and vanilla. Gradually blend in remaining sugar. Add enough cream so frosting can be easily spread.

Variations. For orange frosting, add 2 teaspoons grated orange peel to butter in butter frosting. Stir in orange juice instead of cream—enough so the frosting can be easily spread.
For chocolate frosting, add two 1-ounce squares unsweetened chocolate, melted and cooled, with the egg yolk and vanilla. Blend well and add to butter frosting.
For lemon frosting, add ½ teaspoon grated lemon peel to butter in butter frosting. Stir in lemon juice instead of cream so the frosting can be easily spread.

Makes enough for two 8 or 9-in. layers.

Coffee-toffee sauce

1 c. brown sugar
   (packed)
1½ c. hot strong coffee
2 T. cornstarch
3 T. cold coffee
2 T. butter
2 t. vanilla

Combine brown sugar and hot coffee. Stir over low heat until sugar melts. Blend cornstarch and cold coffee; stir into the hot mixture. Cook and stir until sauce boils and thickens. Remove from heat. Add butter and vanilla; stir until butter dissolves. Serve warm, over squares of warm cake.

Makes 12 servings.

Ice creams and frozen desserts

Ice creams and frozen desserts

The American love affair with ice cream is famous worldwide. From ice cream cones to dazzling banana splits, this old-fashioned tradition is enjoying a new revival today. We have moved away from the air-filled and artifically flavored ice cream bricks of yesteryear, to simple fresh fruit ices, or rich egg and cream ice creams of all kinds and flavors. Technically, ice cream differs from sherbet in the amount of milk and cream it contains, as well as in the egg custard base that is usually found in quality ice creams. Sherbets are generally lighter in flavor and texture, but contain nearly as many calories as ice cream since the sugar content is generally higher. Ices or sorbets are simply mixtures of fresh fruits or flavorings and liquids such as water or fruit juice. The best textured ice creams and sherbets are churned in hand-cranked or electric freezers. Ices and sherbets can be mixed and processesed by the "still-freezing" method. The mixture is poured into shallow metal pans, placed in the freezer until partially frozen, then beaten or processed in a food processor to incorporate air and break up crystals. This freezing and beating process is repeated two or three times, and then the mixture is frozen solid before serving.

The amount of air or "over-run" which is incorporated into an ice cream determines it richness and usually the quality. A quart of excellent home-made ice cream may weigh twice as much as a cheap, commercial type. When no custard or cream base is used, commercial producers may rely on chemical emulsifiers to improve texture. These definitely affect the quality, but do improve the storage life. Homemade ice cream, on the other hand, if it is made with only fresh cream, milk, eggs and natural flavorings, is at its peak and should be used within a day or so. After that, it may become grainy. Ices keep a bit longer since their original texture is icier.

Frozen desserts such as some mousses and parfaits are quite similar to ice cream, but they are not freezer-churned or processed. Most also require whole or separated egg bases and are wonderful desserts that can be prepared in advance of a party—ideal for the busy host or hostess. None will keep for long periods, but will keep for a few days.

Many of the ice creams and frozen desserts in this chapter are enhanced by some of the dessert sauces that are found in the chapter on Candy, confections and dessert sauces.

Chocolate ice cream

⅓ c. water
1 c. sugar
3 egg whites
¼ t. cream of tartar
pinch of salt
2 T. instant espresso
   coffee powder
¼ c. water
1 c. milk
5-oz. sweet chocolate
2-oz. baking chocolate
2 t. vanilla extract
1 c. heavy cream

In a saucepan, combine ⅓ cup water and the sugar, and bring to a boil over medium heat, stirring constantly. Cover and boil the syrup over high heat until it reaches the soft-ball stage, about 238° F. Remove from heat. Beat egg whites until they are foamy. Add cream of tartar and salt; beat until stiff peaks form. Continue to beat while pouring in the syrup in a steady stream until the mixture is thick and shiny. Set aside.

Dissolve the espresso powder in the water and place mixture in a saucepan with the milk. Chop the sweet and baking chocolates finely and add to the milk. Place saucepan over low to medium heat, and cook, stirring, until the chocolate has completely melted. Simmer a few minutes longer, making sure the mixture does not stick to the bottom of the pan. Remove the pan from the heat and set in a bowl of ice. Stir until steam no longer rises from the chocolate mixture. Stir in vanilla extract. Fold the chocolate mixture into the syrup mixture. Whip heavy cream until it just holds its shape. Fold whipped cream into chocolate mixture. Pour into plastic containers. Cover with plastic wrap and put lids on the containers. Freeze until firm.

Makes about 2 quarts.

Vanilla ice cream

4 egg yolks
pinch of salt
½ c. sugar
1 (1-in.) piece vanilla
  bean*
2 c. plus 2 T. milk
1 T. sweet butter
1 c. heavy cream

Beat egg yolks until they are very thick. Add a pinch of salt and the sugar gradually; continue beating until the mixture forms a slowly dissolving ribbon when the beater is lifted.

Slit open the piece of vanilla bean and place it in a nonaluminum saucepan with the milk. Place over moderate heat and bring to a boil. Remove the saucepan from the heat and take out the vanilla bean. Pour the milk over the egg yolk mixture gradually, beating constantly with a wire whisk. Transfer the mixture to a larger saucepan and place it over moderate heat, or place the mixture in the top of a double boiler over hot water. Cook, beating constantly, until the mixture thickens slightly. Do not allow it to boil.

Remove from heat and stir in the butter. Allow the mixture to cool, and stir in the heavy cream. Freeze in a manual or electric ice cream freezer according to the manufacturer's instructions, or place the mixture in freezing trays or plastic containers and freeze until it becomes mushy. Beat with an electric beater until smooth. Freeze again until nearly firm. Beat once more with the electric beater until smooth. Place ice cream in plastic containers, cover tightly, and freeze until firm.

Vanilla bean gives a rich, distinctive vanilla flavor and should be used if at all possible. If it cannot be found, substitute 1½ teaspoons vanilla extract, which should be stirred in with the butter after cooking.

Makes about 1 quart.

Vanilla ice cream converts to...

There are so many good commercially-prepared ice creams in the United States that it makes sense to utilize them in preparing frozen desserts. Using plain vanilla as a base, it is possible to make exotic ice cream flavors that cannot be bought. A number of suggestions follow:

Ginger ice cream

½ c. drained preserved ginger in syrup, very finely chopped
2 T. syrup from ginger jar
1 qt. vanilla ice cream

Combine the chopped ginger with the ginger syrup. Soften the ice cream and quickly stir the ginger mixture into it. Pack the ice cream in plastic containers, cover, and freeze until firm.

Makes about 1 quart.

Macaroon ice cream

1 c. almond macaroon crumbs
2 T. maple syrup, or ½ t. almond extract
1 qt. vanilla ice cream

Crush macaroon crumbs finely, and toss with maple syrup or almond extract. Soften the ice cream and quickly stir the macaroon mixture into it. Pack the ice cream in plastic containers, cover, and freeze until firm.

Makes about 1 quart.

Mango ice cream

1 mango, peeled and cut
   into pieces
1 T. plus 1 t. lime juice
2 T. honey
1 pt. vanilla ice cream

Blend the mango pieces, lime juice, and honey briefly in an electric blender or food processor. Soften the ice cream and quickly stir the mango mixture into it. Pack the ice cream in plastic containers, cover, and freeze until firm.

Makes about 1 scant quart.

Fig ice cream

10 canned green figs,
   drained
2 t. lemon juice
1 qt. vanilla ice cream

Puree figs in electric blender or food processor. Add lemon juice. Soften the ice cream and quickly stir the fig mixture into it. Turn the mixture into a rectangular pan or freezer tray and freeze until slightly firm. Stir well, from the bottom up. Pack the ice cream in plastic containers, cover, and freeze until firm.

Makes about 1 quart.

Persimmon ice cream

6 very ripe persimmons
1 t. lemon juice
1 qt. vanilla ice cream

Peel the persimmons and chop them coarsely, removing any surrounding hard substance and seeds. Combine with lemon juice. Soften the ice cream and quickly stir the persimmon mixture into it. Pack the ice cream in plastic containers, cover, and freeze until firm.

Makes 1 generous quart.

Praline ice cream

½ c. slivered blanched
  almonds
½ c. sugar
3 T. water
⅛ t. cream of tartar
1 qt. vanilla ice cream

Spread the ½ cup of almonds on a baking sheet. Toast them in a moderate oven for 5 to 7 min. until they are lightly browned. Turn them once while toasting. Watch carefully to see that the nuts do not burn.

Combine the sugar, water, and cream of tartar in a small saucepan. Heat, stirring constantly, until the mixture comes to a boil and the sugar has completely dissolved. Stir in the toasted nuts, and cook over medium heat without stirring until the mixture is golden-brown. Pour the praline mixture onto a piece of buttered aluminum foil and allow it to cool. When it has cooled, break it up and crush with a rolling pin or with a mortar and pestle. The pieces can be put through an electric blender or food processor until they have been reduced to powder.

Soften the ice cream and quickly stir the praline mixture into it. Pack the ice cream in plastic containers, cover, and freeze until firm.

Makes about 1 quart.

Apricot ice cream

12 or more canned,
  peeled, pitted apricots
2 t. lemon juice or
  apricot brandy
1 qt. vanilla ice cream
chopped pistachio nuts
  or whipped cream
  and glazed apricot
  pieces (optional)

Puree enough apricots in an electric blender or food processor to measure 1 cup. Add the lemon juice or apricot brandy. Soften the ice cream and quickly stir the apricot mixture into it. Pack the ice cream in plastic containers, cover, and freeze until firm. To serve, spoon the ice cream into dessert glasses and, if desired, decorate with chopped pistachio nuts or whipped cream and glazed apricot pieces.

Makes 1 generous quart.

Bali parfait

1 banana
¾ c. drained
    unsweetened crushed
    pineapple
3 T. unsweetened flaked
    coconut
2 T. brown sugar
¼ t. cinnamon
pinch of mace
1 qt. vanilla ice cream

Mash the banana and combine it with the crushed pineapple, coconut, brown sugar, cinnamon, and mace. Soften the ice cream and quickly stir the banana mixture into it. Pack the ice cream in plastic containers, cover, and freeze until firm.

Makes 1 generous quart.

Cranberry ice cream

2 c. cranberries
1¼ c. sugar
1 pt. vanilla ice cream
whipped cream
    (optional)

Put the cranberries in a buttered shallow baking dish and sprinkle them with the sugar. Cover with aluminum foil and bake 1 hour. Cool. Soften the ice cream and quickly mix in the cooled cranberries, reserving 4 for garnish. Pack the ice cream in plastic containers, cover and freeze until firm. If desired, decorate each serving with dollops of whippped cream and a reserved cranberry.

Preheat oven to 350° F.

Makes 4 servings.

Cantaloupe ice cream

1 or 2 cantaloupes
1 T. honey
1 T. orange liqueur
1 qt. vanilla ice cream

Pare, seed, and cut up the cantaloupes. Put pieces through an electric blender or food processor, pureeing enough to measure 2 cups. Combine with the honey and orange liqueur. Soften the ice cream and quickly stir the melon mixture into it. Pack the ice cream in plastic containers, cover, and freeze until firm.

Makes about 1½ quarts.

THE DESSERT COOKBOOK

English toffee ice cream with praline sauce

3 (1⅛-oz.) chocolate-
 coated English toffee
 bars
1 qt. vanilla ice cream
1 oz. sweet chocolate
½ c. heavy cream

Crush 2 of the candy bars with a rolling pin, or break them up and put through a food processor. Soften the ice cream and quickly stir the crushed toffee into it. Pack the ice cream in plastic containers, cover, and freeze until firm.

Break up the remaining candy bar and place it in a small saucepan with the sweet chocolate and heavy cream. Heat the mixture over a low flame, stirring constantly, until the chocolate has completely melted. Serve it hot or at room temperature, spooned over servings of the ice cream.

Makes about 1 quart of ice cream and enough sauce for 6 servings.

Quick ice cream desserts

Pecan balls. Toast 1½ cups pecans in shallow pan at 300° F. for 15 to 20 min., or until lightly browned. Watch to be sure they do not burn. Cool and chop. Shape 1-quart ice cream into 6 balls. Roll balls in pecans. Place in muffin tins or tray covered with wax paper. Freeze until firm. Just before serving, top balls with hot fudge sauce.

Snowballs. Shape 1-quart ice cream into 6 balls. Roll balls in ½ cup flaked coconut. Freeze as directed above.

Ice cream sandwiches. Slice 1-quart ice cream into 6 slices. Place each slice between 2 graham crackers (plain, cinnamon-flavored, or chocolate-coated). Serve immediately or freeze until time to serve.

Buttered nut sundae. Add ½ cup chopped pecans or walnuts to 2 tablespoons melted butter or margarine in a frying pan. Toast nuts over low heat for 15 to 30 min., stirring as needed, until they are lightly browned. Stir in ¼ cup brown sugar (packed) and ¼ cup water; simmer 2 min. Pour warm sauce over ice cream. Makes about ¾ cup, or enough for 6 sundaes.

Fresh peach ice cream

2 c. crushed ripe
   peaches
1⅓ c. sugar
1 t. almond extract
⅛ t. salt
2 T. flour
2 eggs, slightly beaten
1½ c. milk
2 t. vanilla
2 c. heavy cream

Mix peaches with ½ cup sugar and extract. Set aside. Mix remaining sugar, salt, and flour; blend in eggs and ¼ cup milk. Add remaining milk and cook over low heat, stirring constantly, until mixture coats a metal spoon. Cool. Add vanilla and cream. Pour mixture into freezer trays and freeze until firm ½-in. around edges. Remove from trays and beat vigorously until smooth and fluffy. Fold in peach mixture, return to trays, and freeze until firm.

Makes 1½ quarts.

Frozen lime cream

5 egg yolks
⅔ c. sugar
⅔ c. fresh lime juice
grated peel of 1 lime
5 egg whites
pinch of salt
1 c. heavy cream

Preheat oven to 350° F.

Beat egg yolks in top of double boiler until very thick. Add ⅓ cup sugar gradually, and continue beating until mixture forms a slowly dissolving ribbon when the beater is lifted. Stir in the lime juice and lime peel. Set over hot water and cook, stirring, until the mixture thickens slightly. Be sure it does not boil. Remove from heat and cool to room temperature.

    Beat egg whites with salt until they form soft peaks. Add remaining ⅓ cup sugar gradually, and continue beating until stiff peaks form. Stir a little of the egg white mixture into the egg yolk mixture. Then fold in the rest of the egg white mixture. Turn into a buttered 1-quart souffle dish and bake for 15 min. Cool. Cover tightly with plastic wrap. Chill and then freeze. To serve, whip the heavy cream and swirl it over the entire surface of the lime cream.

Makes 8 servings.

Raspberry cream sherbet

2 (10-oz.) pkg. frozen
  raspberries, thawed
1 T. lemon juice
¾ c. sugar
⅓ c. water
1 T. corn syrup
3 egg whites
pinch of salt
¼ t. cream of tartar
½ c. heavy cream

Puree raspberries in an electric blender or food processor. Put puree through a fine sieve to remove seeds. Add lemon juice. Combine sugar, water, and corn syrup in a saucepan, and bring to a boil, stirring until the sugar has dissolved. Cook to the soft-ball stage, about 238° F.

Beat the egg whites until they are foamy. Add salt and cream of tartar, and continue beating until stiff peaks form. Pour the sugar syrup in a fine stream over the beaten egg whites, beating continually, until well combined. Fold in about ⅓ of the raspberry puree. Whip the heavy cream until it holds its shape but is not too stiff. Fold it into the egg white mixture. Fold in the remaining raspberry puree, ½ at a time, until the mixtures are well combined. Pour into a rectangular pan or freezer tray, and freeze until the mixture becomes mushy, about 1 hour. Stir well, scraping down the sides and the bottom of the pan, until the mixture is completely smooth. Pour the sherbet into plastic containers. Cover with plastic wrap and put lids on the containers. Freeze until firm.

Makes 1 quart.

Vanilla ice cream converts to...

Frozen strawberry mousse

4 c. fresh strawberries
⅔ c. sugar
⅓ c. water
2 egg whites
¼ t. cream of tartar
2 c. heavy cream
1 t. vanilla extract

Puree strawberries in electric blender or food processor. Set aside. In a saucepan combine sugar and water and bring to a boil, stirring constantly. Cover and boil over high heat until the mixture reaches the soft-ball stage, about 238° F. Remove from heat.

Beat the egg whites until they are foamy. Add cream of tartar and beat until stiff peaks form. Continue to beat while pouring in the syrup in a steady stream over the egg whites. Beat until the mixture is thick and glossy. Fold strawberry puree into egg white mixture. Whip heavy cream until stiff. Add vanilla extract. Fold whipped cream into strawberry mixture, combining them well. Pour the mixture into plastic containers, a freezable decorative deep serving dish or bowl, or a collared 1½-quart souffle dish. Cover container tightly with plastic wrap, and seal with lid if available. Freeze for several hours.

To serve, spoon the mousse into serving dishes, unmold on a serving plate, or remove the collar from the souffle dish.

Makes 8 or more servings.

Frozen peppermint mousse

1 lb. peppermint candy canes
2 c. milk
2 c. heavy cream

Crush candy. Soak half the crushed candy in milk overnight. Whip cream stiff and fold into candy mixture. Divide between 2 refrigerator trays and freeze until mushy. Transfer to mixer bowl and beat thoroughly. Add other half crushed candy and freeze until firm.

Makes 8 servings.

Baked Alaska

A Norwegienne, a bombe, an omellette surprise are all names for this ice cream, cake, and meringue dessert. Supposedly created in 1792 by Benjamin Thompson of Massachusetts, later known as Count Rumford of England, to test the heat convection of a hot oven, this show-off specialty proves how insulation works. The cake and meringue protect the ice cream during its quick trip into the oven.

3 pt. ice cream, partially softened
6 egg whites
½ t. cream of tartar
¼ t. salt
¾ c. sugar
1 t. vanilla
1 round sponge or layer cake (8-in.)

Preheat oven to 450° F.

Line 1½-quart round mixing bowl (7 to 8-in. in diameter) with aluminum foil. Press ice cream into bowl and freeze until firm, at least 2 to 3 hours.

Beat egg whites, cream of tartar, and salt at high speed until foamy. Add sugar, 2 tablespoons at a time, beating constantly until sugar is dissolved* and whites are glossy and stand in soft peaks. Blend in vanilla.

Place cake on oven-proof serving plate. Top with prepared ice cream, flat side down. Remove foil. Trim off edge of cake. Working quickly, cover the cake and ice cream completely with meringue, sealing edges tightly to the serving plate. Spread meringue in attractive swirls. Bake on lowest rack in preheated oven until peaks are lightly browned, 3 to 5 min. Serve immediately.

*Rub a bit of meringue between thumb and forefinger to be sure sugar has dissolved.

Makes 8 to 10 servings.

Vanilla ice cream converts to...

Candies, confections, and sauces

Candies, confections, and sauces

Cooked candies are a bit tricky, but most satisfying, to make. Their success depends upon an understanding of the sugar cooking process. An accurate candy thermometer is most desirable and far better than the old-fashioned testing method of dropping a ball into iced water. Even a few degrees of variation can make the difference between a fudge that won't set up at all, sets up like a rock, and one that is firm, creamy, and smooth. In candy making, you are converting solid sugars like granulated and brown sugar, into a liquid or *invert* sugar that is cooked to the proper stage and will not become grainy. Between 234° and 240° F. a sugar syrup will solidify when cooled but will remain creamy and smooth. This is the appropriate temperature range for fudge. Caramels and taffy are cooked a bit further—between 242° and 265° F. They are still creamy, but become chewy. The higher temperature is required for taffy which is meant to be harder in texture than a soft, caramel candy. Between 265° and 300° F. the syrup will harden and when cooled become very brittle. Toffees, peanut brittles, and hard candies are good examples of this. In all cases, the temperature reflects a certain amount of moisture that is evaporated from the syrup and thus it is especially difficult to make candy on humid or rainy days.

When beginning the syrup making process, the mixture should be brought slowly to a boil and stirred constantly to dissolve sugar crystals. As soon as the mixture boils, use a damp brush to wipe down any undissolved sugar from the sides of the pan, or the candy may become grainy and re-crystallize after cooking. Then allow the syrup and any added ingredients to cook undisturbed until it reaches the proper temperature. After 220° F., the temperature changes rapidly, so watch closely. Always use a pot that is at least four times the capacity of the ingredients since boiling sugar syrup bubbles and foams at a rapid rate. Beaten candies, such as fudge, should

Candies, confections, and sauces   111

be allowed to cool in the pan undisturbed until it is lukewarm or about 110° F. which may take up to an hour. Watch carefully though, because if it cools too much, it will be difficult to beat. Once it's ready, beat the mixture only until it begins to lose its gloss and then pour immediately into the prepared pan. It should set in a matter of minutes. Only pour the liquid candy mixture that falls easily from the pot. The coating left on the bottom is probably overcooked and will contain some granular sugar. If you scrape this into the candy, the entire mixture may become grainy. All candies should be stored in airtight containers. Avoid refrigeration, which will introduce moisture. Very hard candies, such as peanut brittle, will stay fresh up to a month and soft candies, such as fudge, will keep for at least a week.

Dessert sauces often fall into the cooked candy category although they are rarely heated above the boiling point. Some of the most simple sauces are simply uncooked fresh fruit purées and are wonderful over ice cream and plain cakes. Custard sauces rely upon eggs for thickening and must be cooked over gentle heat or in the top of a double boiler to prevent curdling. Chocolate burns easily, so fudge sauces must also be carefully and gently cooked. Cooked sauces, such as butterscotch and caramel, depend upon the same sugar dissolving techniques and temperature control as candy. A butterscotch sauce can be very liquid at a low temperature, but can become sticky and caramel-like if heated higher. Follow recipe cooking times and monitor well.

The sauces included in this chapter are versatile toppings for ice creams, cakes and even some pies. Most cooked sauces and custards keep well for a few days in the refrigerator, but fruit purees are best eaten soon after making.

Coconut fudge

3 c. fresh-grated coconut
½ c. milk
2½ c. sugar
1 T. ground cinnamon or ginger
7–8 cardamon seeds, ground
1 t. vanilla

Mix coconut, milk, and sugar in deep frying pan. Brown on low heat, stirring constantly. When golden-brown and beginning to harden, quickly add ginger or cinnamon, cardamon, and vanilla. Pour mixture onto a greased tray. When set, cut into pieces and serve. May also be formed into balls.

Makes about 3 dozen pieces.

French fudge

3 c. semi-sweet chocolate pieces
1 can sweetened condensed milk
pinch of salt
1½ t. vanilla
½ c. ground nutmeats (optional)

In top of double boiler melt chocolate over hot water; stir a few times. Remove from heat. Stir in sweetened condensed milk, salt, vanilla, and nuts, if used. Stir only until smooth. Turn into pan; spread evenly and smoothly. Allow to set (2 hours in refrigerator or 5–6 hours at room temperature). Turn candy onto cutting board, peel off paper, and cut into squares.

Makes about 1 pound.

Line an 8x8-in. pan with waxed paper.

Chocolate nut fudge

½ c. milk
2 c. sugar
1 T. butter
1 T. cocoa
vanilla to taste
chopped nuts (optional)

Put milk, sugar, butter, and cocoa in a saucepan and bring to a boil. Boil 4 min. Remove from heat and add vanilla. Nuts should be added if they are used. Beat until thick and pour into a buttered dish. Cut when set.

Makes about 2 dozen pieces.

Candies, confections, and sauces

Chocolate fudge

2 c. sugar
¾ c. cream or milk
2 T. corn syrup
2-oz. unsweetened
  chocolate or 4 T.
  cocoa & 2 T. butter
1 t. vanilla

Lightly butter an 8x8-in.
  loaf pan.

In a heavy saucepan over moderate heat, stir all ingredients until chocolate melts. Cook on low heat to soft-ball stage, approximately 234° F.; remove from heat. Add 2 tablespoons of butter; do not stir. Let mixture stand until almost cold. Add 1 teaspoon of vanilla. Beat until no longer glossy, and fudge is thick and creamy. Pour into pan.

For chocolate peanut butter fudge, substitute 1 tablespoon peanut butter for 1 tablespoon of butter. (To test for soft-ball stage, drop a small amount of mixture into cold water. Mixture will flatten but not disintegrate.) Pour into pan.

Makes about 2 pounds.

Divinity fudge

2½ c. sugar
½ c. corn syrup
½ c. water
2 egg whites

Cook syrup, sugar, and water until it forms a thread, then pour half of this mixture into stiffly beaten egg whites. Beat thoroughly. Cook the other half longer, until it hardens in cold water. Add this half to other mixture and beat until creamy. Pour into a buttered pan or drop by spoonfuls on waxed or brown paper.

Makes about 4 dozen pieces.

Vanilla divinity fudge

It's the beaten egg whites that make this candy different from others that start with boiled syrup. A candy thermometer is a helpful guide for accurate cooking. The resulting candy is as white and airy as an angel's wing.

2½ c. sugar
½ c. light corn syrup
½ c. water
¼ t. salt
3 egg whites
1 t. vanilla

In medium saucepan combine sugar, corn syrup, water, and salt. Cook, stirring constantly, over medium heat until sugar is dissolved. Bring to a boil and, without stirring, continue cooking until mixture reaches 260° F. on a candy thermometer or the hard-ball stage.

In large mixing bowl beat egg whites at high speed until stiff but not dry, just until whites no longer slip when bowl is tilted. Continue beating at high speed and slowly pour hot syrup over egg whites. Do not scrape saucepan. Beat at high speed until mixture holds its shape when dropped from a spoon, 4 to 5 min. Beat in vanilla. Working quickly, drop a teaspoonful at a time onto waxed paper, aluminum foil, or greased cookie sheets. Cool.

Variations If desired, ¼ cup chopped nuts, toasted coconut, raisins, chopped pitted dates, or candied fruits may be stirred into candy just before dropping onto waxed paper.

Makes about 4½ dozen pieces.

Candied ginger

1 c. fresh ginger root
½ c. sugar
¼ c. sugar
¼ c. water

Wash, scrape, and slice ginger root into thin slices. Cover with cold water and boil for 5 min. Drain. Cover again with cold water and boil another 5 min. Drain, then spread ginger pieces on clean dry towel. Prepare syrup by combining ½ cup sugar and the water. Stir until sugar dissolves. Cook over low flame until syrup thickens. Add ginger slices and cook over low heat until syrup is absorbed. Allow ginger slices to dry for at least an hour. Roll in sugar. Let stand until sugar crystallizes. Store in airtight jars.

Makes 1 cup.

Kookie brittle

1 c. margarine
1½ t. vanilla
1 t. salt
1 c. sugar
2 c. sifted flour
1 (6-oz.) pkg. chocolate
   chips
1 c. chopped walnuts

Combine margarine, vanilla, and salt; blend well. Gradually beat in sugar. Blend in flour. Add chocolate chips and ¾ cup of the walnuts; mix well. Press evenly into an ungreased 15x10x1-in. pan. Sprinkle remaining nuts over top and press in lightly. Bake about 25 min., or until golden-brown. Cool; break into irregular pieces.

Makes about 2 pounds.

Preheat oven to 375° F.

Vanilla sauce

4 T. butter
4 T. flour
pinch of salt
6 T. sugar
4 c. milk
2 t. vanilla

Melt butter in a small saucepan, remove from heat. Add the flour and mix well. Add milk, salt, and sugar; return to heat. Bring to a boil, stirring constantly. Add vanilla, stir again, and cool. Serve over pies, gingerbread, apple crisp, and other desserts where appropriate.

Makes 4½ cups.

Strawberry sauce

1 pt. fresh strawberries
1 or 2 T. sugar
2 T. orange juice
1 t. grated lemon peel
1 t. grated orange peel

Hull strawberries and slice in half lengthwise. Sprinkle with sugar; add remaining ingredients. Allow to stand 15 min. or longer. Serve over vanilla ice cream.

Makes about 4 cups.

Chocolate sauce

1¼ c. sugar
pinch of salt
1 c. heavy cream
3-oz. baking chocolate, chopped
1 t. vanilla extract

Combine sugar, salt, heavy cream, and chocolate in a small saucepan and cook over medium heat, stirring constantly, until the chocolate has melted. Increase the heat and bring to a boil. Cook, stirring, until the mixture reaches the soft-ball stage, about 238° F. Remove from heat and stir in the vanilla extract. Serve hot or at room temperature.

Chocolate sauce may be used as a cake frosting, in which case it should be spooned over the cake while warm. It may be served as a sauce on frozen desserts, custards, or any dessert where chocolate sauce could be used.

Makes about 3 cups.

Heavenly chocolate sauce

1 can evaporated milk
   (14½-oz.)
2 c. sugar
3 squares chocolate (3-
   oz.)
vanilla

In a double boiler, combine milk, sugar, and chocolate. Cook over simmering water about 15 min., stirring occasionally, until chocolate melts. Remove from heat, and add vanilla. Beat with beater until smooth and thick. Serve sauce hot or cold over ice cream.

Makes about 2¾ cups.

Sauce for berries

½ pt. sour cream
crumbled macaroons
2 T. brown sugar

Mix together. Let stand in refrigerator at least 3 hours. Serve in bowl on platter of assorted berries.

Makes 2 cups.

Bing cherry sauce

1 can pitted bing
   cherries (17-oz.)
2 T. cornstarch
⅛ t. salt
1 t. lemon juice
½ t. almond extract
   (optional)

Drain cherries. Add enough water to syrup to make 1½ cups. Blend syrup, cornstarch, and salt. Cook and stir until thickened and clear. Add cherries, lemon juice and, if desired, the almond extract. Cool.

Makes about 3 cups.

Butterscotch sauce

1¼ c. light brown sugar
⅔ c. corn syrup
4 T. butter
¾ c. thin cream

Mix together the sugar, corn syrup, and butter. Bring to boil, stirring constantly, and cook to 228° F. Add cream and mix well.

Makes about 3 cups.

Fudge sauce

1 c. sugar
¾ c. milk
½ T. butter
2 T. cocoa or 6 T. grated chocolate
½ t. vanilla extract
1 T. corn syrup (or more)

Mix the sugar, milk, butter, cocoa or chocolate and cook, stirring constantly, until the mixture boils. Continue to cook without stirring for about 6 min., or just before the mixture reaches the soft-ball stage of 220° F. Add ½ teaspoon vanilla and a tablespoon or more of corn syrup to prevent hardening. Serve over ice cream.

Makes about 2 cups.

Cookies

Cookies

Everyone loves cookies! Throughout the world Christmas cookies are a major tradition. It seems as though Americans could not survive without chocolate chip cookies and a glass of cold milk from time-to-time. More than a dessert, cookies make wonderful snacks, lunch box treats and gifts for almost any occasion. In fact, cookies are terrific anytime.

Cookie preparation ranges in difficulty from the simplest of sugar cookies to the most complicated of rolled and filled morsels, traditional to many celebrations. Types of cookies fall into relatively neat categories and a beautiful assorted tray could include some of each. Drop cookies probably require the least amount of time and are the most "homespun" in appearance. Refrigerator doughs are formed into rolls or logs and are then chilled up to a week and can be frozen for about three months. When you're ready to bake them, simply slice the chilled or partially frozen dough with a sharp knife. Rolled cookies also use chilled dough for easier handling and are cut into any number of fanciful shapes and sizes from tiny sugar cookies to giant gingerbread men. Pressed cookies are usually made from a plain butter-rich dough that is pushed through a manual or electric press. These include the marvelous Spritz cookies so integral to German Christmases. Filled cookies can be made from rolled dough and shaped into turnovers or crescents as well as other shapes. They can also be baked as thin wafers and, after cooling, sandwiched together with filling. Bar cookies, such as brownies, are more cake-like than the others, but have the advantage of one-pan baking and require no rolling, cutting or shaping. They usually keep quite well, too.

When making cookies, start with room temperature ingredients unless the recipe specifies otherwise. Most recipes today are tested using "large" graded eggs and double-acting baking powder. Bake in the center of a preheated oven on a shiny steel or aluminum baking sheet for best results. Black steel pans are good but tend to retain heat and promote over-browning of the bottoms. Avoid baking on two racks at a time, but if you must do so, be sure to alternate the sheets halfway through the baking time. Unless the recipe states otherwise, remove all cookies except bars from the baking sheet as soon as they are cool enough to handle—usually within a minute—or they will continue to bake on the hot sheets. It is not necessary to re-grease the sheets between bakings, but be sure to let them cool completely. Allow baked cookies to cool thoroughly before storing.

Most cookies should be stored in airtight containers to keep the texture moist. Soft cookies can be stored with a small slice of apple which will help to prevent drying. Most cookies, with the exception of meringues, freeze well and thaw quickly. In addition, most unbaked doughs lend themselves well to freezing. If you plan to decorate the cookies with powdered sugar or a thin icing, do so after they are thawed. Even buttercream or jam filled cookies will keep for a long time in the freezer.

Cookies are versatile because they are easy to prepare and will keep for a relatively long time. This makes them a wonderfully sweet snack or dessert to have on hand for all occasions.

Applesauce drop cookies

½ c. butter or
   margarine
1 c. sugar
1 egg
1 c. flour, unsifted
1½ t. baking powder
½ t. salt
1 t. cinnamon
¼ t. ground cloves
½ t. ground nutmeg
1 c. applesauce
1 c. raisins
1½ c. quick-cooking
   rolled oats, uncooked

Preheat oven to 375° F.
Grease baking sheet.

Beat shortening and sugar until creamy. Beat in egg. Mix flour, baking powder, salt, and spices thoroughly; stir into shortening mixture. Stir in applesauce, raisins, and rolled oats. Drop by level tablespoonfuls onto cookie sheet. Bake about 15 min. or until edges are slightly browned.

Makes 5 dozen cookies.

Ginger snaps

¾ c. butter or
   margarine, softened
1 c. sugar
1 egg
⅓ c. light molasses
2 c. flour, unsifted
1 t. baking soda
½ t. salt
1 t. cloves
1 t. cinnamon
1 t. ginger

Preheat oven to 375° F.
Grease cookie sheet.

Mix shortening, sugar, and egg together until creamy. Stir in molasses. Mix flour, baking soda, salt, and spices. Stir into molasses mixture and mix well. Roll dough into 60 balls, ¾ to 1-in. in diameter. Place about 2 in. apart on cookie sheet. Bake 10 to 12 min. or until lightly browned. Remove from baking sheet while still warm. Cool on rack.

Makes 5 dozen cookies.

Frosted ginger cookies

¼ c. shortening
½ c. sugar
1 egg
⅓ c. light molasses
2 c. flour, unsifted
½ t. baking soda
½ t. salt
1¼ t. powdered ginger
½ t. cinnamon
½ t. cloves
½ c. water

Mix shortening and sugar until creamy. Add egg; beat well. Stir in molasses. Mix flour, baking soda, salt, and spices thoroughly. Add to molasses mixture alternately with ½ cup water. Drop by teaspoonfuls onto cookie sheet about 2-in. apart. Bake 10 min. or until lightly browned. Remove from baking sheet while still warm. Cool on rack.

frosting
1¼ c. confectioners' sugar
1–2 T. water

To make the frosting, mix confectioners' sugar with enough water to make a stiff but spreadable frosting. Spread about ½ teaspoon of frosting on each cookie.

Makes 5 dozen cookies.

Preheat oven to 350° F.
Grease cookie sheet.

THE DESSERT COOKBOOK

Sour cream cookies

½ c. butter or
  margarine, softened
1 c. sugar
2 eggs, beaten
1 t. vanilla
1¾ c. flour, unsifted
½ t. salt
¼ t. baking soda
½ t. nutmeg
½ c. sour cream
1 c. nuts, chopped

Beat shortening and sugar together until creamy. Beat in eggs and vanilla. Stir flour, salt, baking soda, and nutmeg together. Mix flour mixture, sour cream, and nuts with shortening mixture. Drop dough from a teaspoon onto cookie sheets; space cookies about 2-in. apart. Bake 10 to 12 min., or until lightly browned around the edges.

Makes 4 dozen cookies.

Preheat oven to 375° F.
Grease 2 baking sheets.

Refrigerator cookies

1 c. butter or margarine,
  softened
1½ c. sugar
2 eggs
2 t. lemon or vanilla
  extract
3 c. flour, unsifted
2 t. baking powder
½ t. salt

Mix shortening and sugar until creamy. Add eggs and flavoring; beat well. Mix flour, baking powder, and salt thoroughly. Add to creamy mixture. Mix well. Chill dough 1 hour. Form into 3 rolls about 9-in. long. Wrap rolls tightly in wax paper or plastic wrap. Chill rolls thoroughly.
Preheat oven to 375° F. Remove rolls of dough from refrigerator; unwrap. Slice dough ⅛ to ¼-in. thick. Place slices about 1-in. apart on baking sheet. Bake 10 min. or until lightly browned. Remove from baking sheet while still warm. Cool on rack.

Grease cookie sheet.

Makes 10 dozen cookies.

Black walnut refrigerator cookies

¾ c. butter or
  margarine, softened
1½ c. brown sugar,
  packed
2 eggs, beaten
1 t. vanilla
2⅔ c. flour, unsifted
2 t. baking powder
½ t. salt
1 c. black walnuts,
  chopped

Mix shortening and sugar until creamy. Add eggs and vanilla; beat well. Mix flour, baking powder, and salt thoroughly; add to creamy mixture. Add nuts and mix well. Chill dough 1 hour. Form dough into 3 rolls about 8-in. long. Wrap rolls tightly in wax paper or plastic wrap. Chill rolls thoroughly.

Preheat oven to 375° F. Remove rolls of dough from refrigerator, one at a time; unwrap. Slice dough ⅛ to ¼-in. thick. Place slices about 1-in. apart on cookie sheet. Bake 10 min., or until lightly browned. Remove from cookie sheet while still warm. Cool on rack.

Makes 9 dozen cookies.

Grease cookie sheet.

Pecan party cookies

1 c. butter or margarine,
  softened
½ c. sugar
2 egg yolks
1 t. vanilla
2⅔ c. flour, unsifted
2 egg whites, unbeaten
1½ c. pecans, finely
  chopped

frosting
1 c. confectioners' sugar
1 T. water
food coloring, as desired

Mix shortening and sugar until creamy. Add egg yolks and vanilla and beat well. Add flour; mix well. Dough will be stiff. Divide dough into 60 balls about 1-in. in diameter. Roll each ball in egg whites then in nuts. Each should be well coated. Place balls on cookie sheet, about 2-in. apart. Press with bottom of a glass until about ½-in. thick. Bake 5 min. Remove from oven. Make a slight indentation in center of each cookie. Return to oven and bake 15 min. longer. Remove from baking sheet while still warm. Cool on rack. Mix confectioners' sugar and water to make thick frosting. Color as desired. Fill indentations in each cookie with frosting.

Makes 5 dozen cookies.

Preheat oven to 350° F.
Grease cookie sheet.

THE DESSERT COOKBOOK

Banana-peanut butter cookies

1¼ c. sifted flour
½ t. baking powder
¼ t. baking soda
¼ t. salt
½ c. butter or
  margarine, softened
½ c. peanut butter
1 c. sugar
¼ c. mashed bananas

Sift dry ingredients. Cream shortening, peanut butter, and sugar; add banana, then flour mixture. Mix well. Roll into 1-in. balls and flatten into crisscross patterns with fork tines. Place on cookie sheet, and bake for 12 min.

Makes 4 dozen cookies.

Preheat oven to 375° F.
Grease cookie sheet.

Peanut butter bars

⅓ c. butter or
  margarine, softened
½ c. chunky peanut
  butter
1 c. brown sugar, packed
2 eggs
½ t. vanilla
1 c. flour, unsifted
1 t. baking powder
¼ t. salt

Mix shortening, peanut butter, and sugar until creamy. Beat in eggs and vanilla. Mix flour, baking powder, and salt thoroughly. Stir into creamy mixture. Spread batter in pan. Bake 30 to 35 min. or until firm in the center. Cool on rack. Cut into bars while still warm.

Makes 24 bars.

Preheat oven to 350° F.
Grease a 9x9x2-in.
  baking pan.

Peanut whirls

½ c. butter
½ c. peanut butter
1 c. sugar
1 egg
1 t. vanilla
1¼ c. flour
½ t. soda
½ t. salt
2 T. milk
6-oz. chocolate bar (or
  6 T. cocoa)

Cream butter, peanut butter, sugar, egg, and vanilla. Sift flour, soda, and salt. Add alternately with milk to creamed mixture. Depending on type of peanut butter used, 1 to 2 extra tablespoons of flour may be needed so the dough will be manageable for rolling. Chill dough for 1 hour. Roll out on floured paper to form a 12x8-in. rectangle. Melt chocolate over hot water, cool slightly, and spread on dough. Roll up lengthwise and chill for 30 min. Slice into ⅛-in. slices. Place on ungreased cookie sheet.
    Bake at 350° F. for 8 to 10 min.

Makes 4 dozen.

Peanut butter cluster cookies

2 c. sifted all-purpose
  flour
2 t. baking powder
½ t. salt
⅔ c. peanut butter
1 egg, slightly beaten
1 can sweetened
  condensed milk
  (15-oz.)
1 t. vanilla
½ c. finely-chopped nut
  meats

Sift together all dry ingredients. In large mixing bowl, blend peanut butter and egg. Stir in half the sweetened condensed milk; blend in half the dry ingredients. Repeat. Stir in vanilla and nut meats. Drop by tablespoonfuls, about 2-in. apart, onto the baking sheet. Bake until cookie edges are lightly browned, 10 to 12 min. Remove from cookie sheet immediately and cool on racks.

Makes 4 dozen cookies.

Preheat oven to 350° F.
Grease well a baking
  sheet.

THE DESSERT COOKBOOK

Peanut butter crunchies

1 c. butter or margarine
⅔ c. chunk-style peanut
   butter
1 c. brown sugar, packed
1 egg
1 t. vanilla
1⅓ c. sifted flour
½ t. soda
¼ t. salt
¾ c. crushed Wheaties

Blend butter and peanut butter; mix in sugar. Stir in egg and vanilla; beat well. Blend flour, soda, and salt; mix thoroughly into butter-sugar mixture. Refrigerate dough several hours or until firm.

    Heat oven to 350° F. Shape dough into small balls; roll in crushed Wheaties. Place about 2-in. apart on greased baking sheet. Bake 12 to 15 min.

Makes 4 dozen cookies.

Grease baking sheet.

Chocolate-peanut cookies

½ c. butter
½ c. sugar
1 egg
1 c. flour
2 t. baking powder
2 T. cocoa
½ lb. peanuts
½ t. salt

Cream butter and sugar; add egg and beat well. Mix in sifted dry ingredients. Add peanuts, and mix well again. Drop by teaspoonfuls onto baking sheet. Bake 20 min.; cool on racks.

Makes about 3 dozen cookies.

Preheat oven to 375° F.
Grease cookie sheet.

Butterscotch brownies

1 pkg. butterscotch chips
(6-oz.)
¼ c. butter or
margarine
1 c. light brown sugar,
packed
2 eggs
½ t. vanilla
1 c. sifted flour
1 t. baking powder
¾ t. salt
½ c. chopped nuts
(optional)

Melt chips over hot (not boiling) water with butter or margarine. Remove from heat. Stir in brown sugar. Blend in eggs and vanilla. Sift together and stir in flour, baking powder and salt. Sitr the nuts into the batter, if used. Spread batter in pan and bake for 25 min. Cool and cut in squares. Nuts can also be spread over top of batter before baking.

Makes 2 dozen brownies.

Preheat oven to 350° F.
Grease and lightly flour
13x9x2-in. pan.

Shortbread

¾ c. butter or
margarine, softened
½ c. sugar
2 c. unsifted flour
¼ t. salt

Mix shortening and sugar until creamy. Mix flour and salt, and add to creamy mixture. Mix until smooth. Press mixture into an ungreased 10x15-in. baking pan. Mixture will be about ¼-in. thick. Bake 20 min., or until very lightly browned. Cut into squares while still warm.

Preheat oven to 350° F.

Variation: For orange or lemon shortbread, add ½ teaspoon grated orange rind or lemon rind to creamy mixture. To make oat shortbread, use only 1⅓ cups unsifted flour. Add ⅔ cup quick-cooking rolled oats to flour mixture.

Makes 24 squares.

Super brownies

2 (1-oz.) squares
   unsweetened
   chocolate
1 c. sugar
½ c. melted butter
⅛ t. salt
2 eggs, separated
½ c. flour
½ c. chopped nuts
1 t. vanilla

Melt chocolate. Add sugar, butter, and salt. Add beaten egg yolks, flour, vanilla, and nuts. Mix well. Fold in stiffly beaten egg whites. Bake in an 8-in. square pan for 20 min. Cool.

frosting for brownies
2 (1-oz.) squares bitter
   chocolate
¼ c. cream
1½ T. butter
1 c. sugar
1 egg, beaten slightly
½ t. vanilla

Melt chocolate. Mix chocolate, cream, butter, sugar, and egg in heavy pan. Bring to a boil, stirring often. Boil 1 min., stirring. Remove from heat, add vanilla, and cool. Beat 2 or 3 min. Spread on brownies and refrigerate overnight. Cut into squares.

Makes 16 brownies.

Preheat oven to 350° F.

Butter horn cookies

2 c. sifted flour
1 t. baking powder
¼ t. salt
½ c. butter
½ pkg. active dry yeast
    (1½ t.)
2 T. warm water
2 eggs, separated
¼ c. commercial sour
    cream
½ t. vanilla
½ c. granulated sugar
½ c. finely ground
    walnuts or pecans
½ t. almond extract
confectioners' sugar

Stir flour, baking powder, and salt together in mixing bowl. Cut in butter. Dissolve yeast in water; stir in egg yolks, sour cream, and vanilla. Blend into flour mixture. Refrigerate 1 hour.

Heat oven to 400° F. Beat egg whites until foamy; gradually add sugar; beat until stiff. Fold in nuts and almond extract. Divide dough in 4 parts. Roll each part into a 9-in. circle on board sprinkled with confectioners' sugar. Cut each circle in 12 wedges. Spread 1 heaping teaspoonful meringue on each. Roll, beginning at wide end. Bake 10 to 12 min., or until golden-brown. Sprinkle with confectioners' sugar.

Makes 4 dozen cookies.

Lightly grease baking
    sheet.

Butter pecan cookies

¾ c. (1½ sticks)
    unsalted butter
1 c. pecans, chopped
    very fine
4 T. powdered sugar
1 T. ice water
2 c. flour
2 t. vanilla
additional powdered
    sugar

Cream together butter and sugar; mix in flour and pecans. Add ice water and mix well; add vanilla and mix again. Roll into small balls and place on ungreased cookie sheets. Bake 20 min. or until cookies just begin to brown. Roll them in additional powdered sugar while still warm. These are very good with ice cream.

Makes 5 dozen cookies.

Preheat oven to 375° F.

THE DESSERT COOKBOOK

Almond butter cookies

1 c. butter
½ c. sugar
1 c. finely chopped
 almonds (do not
 remove skins)
2 t. vanilla
2 c. sifted flour

Cream butter and sugar together. Stir in almonds and vanilla. Blend in flour with pastry blender. Form in small balls (scant teaspoonfuls). Place on ungreased cookie sheet. Flatten with bottom of greased glass dipped in sugar. Bake 9 to 10 min., or until slightly browned.

Makes 6 dozen cookies.

Preheat oven to 350° F.

Sugar and spice cookies

¾ c. shortening
1 c. granulated sugar
1 egg
¼ c. molasses
2 c. sifted flour
2 t. soda
¼ t. salt
1 t. cinnamon
¾ t. cloves
¾ t. ginger
confectioners' sugar

Mix shortening, sugar, egg, and molasses thoroughly. Blend dry ingredients; stir into shortening mixture. Form into 1-in. balls. Place about 2-in. apart on cookie sheet. Bake 10 to 12 min. Roll in confectioners' sugar while still warm.

Makes 4 to 5 dozen cookies.

Preheat oven to 375° F.
Grease cookie sheet.

Cookies

Chocolate crinkles

½ c. vegetable oil
4 (1-oz.) squares
    unsweetened
    chocolate, melted
2 c. granulated sugar
4 eggs
2 t. vanilla
2 c. sifted flour
2 t. baking powder
½ t. salt
1 c. confectioners' sugar

Mix oil, chocolate, and granulated sugar. Blend in one egg at a time until well mixed. Stir vanilla, flour, baking powder, and salt into oil mixture. Chill several hours or overnight.

Heat oven to 350° F. Drop teaspoonfuls of dough into confectioners' sugar. Roll in sugar; shape into balls. Place about 2-in. apart on greased baking sheet. Bake 10 to 12 min. Do not overbake!

Makes 6 dozen cookies.

Grease baking sheet.

Sugar cookies

1½ c. sifted
    confectioners' sugar
1 c. butter or margarine
1 egg
1 t. vanilla
½ t. almond flavoring
2½ c. sifted flour
1 t. soda
1 t. cream of tartar

Mix sugar and butter. Add egg and flavorings; mix thoroughly. Stir dry ingredients together and blend in. Refrigerate 2 to 3 hours.

Heat oven to 375° F. Divide dough in half and roll 3/16-in. thick on lightly floured pastry cloth. Cut with cookie cutter; sprinkle with sugar. Bake 7 to 8 min., or until delicately golden.

Makes 5 dozen 2-in. cookies.

Lightly grease baking
    sheet.

Cinnamon sugar cookies

1 c. softened butter or
  margarine
1¼ c. sugar
2 eggs
½ t. vanilla
2⅔ c. flour
1 t. cinnamon
2 t. cream of tartar
1 t. baking soda
½ t. salt
¼ c. sugar

Beat shortening and sugar until creamy. Beat in eggs; add vanilla. Mix flour, cinnamon, cream of tartar, soda, and salt. Stir into eggs and vanilla; blend well. Chill dough.

Preheat oven to 400° F. Shape dough into balls about 1-in. in diameter. Roll balls in ¼ cup sugar and place about 2-in. apart on an ungreased cookie sheet. Bake 8 to 10 min. Remove from cookie sheet while still warm.

Makes 5 to 6 dozen cookies.

Raisin-honey drop cookies

¾ c. honey
¾ c. sugar
¾ c. butter or
  margarine
1 egg
2 c. flour
½ t. baking soda
1 t. salt
1 t. cinnamon
2 c. uncooked quick-
  rolled oats
1 c. raisins

Mix honey, sugar, and shortening until crumbly. Add egg and beat well. Mix flour, baking soda, salt, and cinnamon. Stir into egg mixture. Mix in the rolled oats and raisins. Drop dough by teaspoonfuls onto the baking sheet. Bake on upper shelf in oven 12 to 14 min. until lightly browned. Remove from pan and cool on rack.

Makes 4 dozen cookies.

Preheat oven to 375° F.
Grease baking sheet.

Jumbo raisin cookies

1 c. water
2 c. seedless raisins
1 c. shortening
2 c. sugar
3 eggs, beaten
1 t. vanilla
1 c. chopped nuts
  (optional)
4 c. sifted flour
1 t. baking powder
1 t. baking soda
2 t. salt
1½ t. cinnamon
½ t. nutmeg
¼ t. allspice

Boil water and raisins together for 5 min. Let cool. Cream shortening and sugar; add eggs and beat well. Add vanilla and cooled raisin mixture, and nuts, if desired. Sift together the flour, baking powder, soda, salt, and spices. Add to the raisin mixture and blend well. Drop by heaping teaspoonfuls on baking sheet and bake for 15 min.

Note: This recipe makes jumbo cookies. Reduce baking time for smaller cookies.

Makes 4 dozen cookies.

Preheat oven to 375° F.
Grease baking sheet.

Coconut nut drops

1 c. butter
1 c. brown sugar
2 eggs
1½ c. flour
1 t. baking powder
1 t. salt
1 t. almond extract
2 c. flaked coconut
1 c. chopped walnuts
candied cherries
  (optional)

Cream butter; add brown sugar and beat until fluffy. Add eggs and beat well. Mix in flour, baking powder, and salt. Add last three ingredients. Place by teaspoonfuls on baking sheet. Add a small piece of candied cherry on top of each cookie, if desired. Bake for 12 to 15 min.

Makes 3 dozen cookies.

Preheat oven to 375° F.

Oatmeal tollhouse cookies

1 c. shortening
¾ c. packed brown
  sugar
¾ c. sugar
2 eggs
1 t. vanilla
1 t. baking soda
1 t. hot water
1 t. salt
1½ c. flour
2 c. quick-cooking oats
1 c. chopped nuts
1 pkg. semi-sweet
  chocolate chips
  (6-oz.)

Cream shortening and sugars until fluffy. Add eggs, one at a time, beating well after each addition. Add vanilla. Dissolve baking soda in the hot water and add to mixture. Sift the salt and flour together and add to mixture. Add oats, nuts, and chocolate chips. Drop by half teaspoonfuls onto baking sheet. Bake for 10 to 12 min.

Makes 3 dozen cookies.

Preheat oven to 350° F.
Lightly grease baking
  sheet.

Snickerdoodles

1 c. shortening
1½ c. sugar
2 eggs
2¾ c. flour
2 t. cream of tartar
1 t. baking soda
½ t. salt
2 T. sugar
2 T. cinnamon

Combine first three ingredients and mix well. Sift together next four ingredients and add to mixture. Chill dough. Roll into walnut-size balls. Roll the balls in mixture of 2 tablespoons sugar and 2 tablespoons cinnamon. Place 2-in. apart on ungreased cookie sheet. Bake 8 to 10 min. at 400° F.

Makes 3 dozen cookies.

Chocolate chip cookies

⅔ c. shortening (part butter or margarine)
½ c. granulated sugar
½ c. brown sugar, packed
1 egg
1 t. vanilla
1½ c. flour
½ t. soda
½ t. salt
½ c. chopped nuts
1 pkg. semi-sweet chocolate pieces (6-oz.)

Mix shortening, sugars, egg, and vanilla thoroughly. (For a softer rounded cookie, add ¼ cup more flour.) Stir dry ingredients together; blend into creamy mixture. Mix in nuts and chocolate pieces. Drop rounded teaspoonfuls of dough about 2-in. apart on ungreased baking sheet. Bake 8 to 10 min., or until delicately browned. (Cookies should still be soft.) Cool slightly before removing from baking sheet.

Makes 4 to 5 dozen cookies.

Preheat oven to 375° F.

Chocolate-kiss cookies

2⅔ c. sifted flour
2 t. baking soda
1 t. salt
1 c. soft butter
⅔ c. creamy peanut butter (room temperature)
1 c. sugar
1 c. brown sugar, firmly packed
2 eggs
2 t. vanilla
5 dozen chocolate kisses

Beat butter and peanut butter at medium speed until well blended. Add sugar and brown sugar; beat until light and fluffy. Add eggs and vanilla; beat until smooth. Stir in sifted dry ingredients until well combined. Using level tablespoonful of batter, shape into 5 dozen balls. Roll in granulated sugar. Place 2-in. apart on ungreased cookie sheet. Bake for 8 min., remove from oven. Press an unwrapped chocolate kiss in top of each cookie. Bake 2 min. longer. Remove cookies to racks to cool.

Makes approximately 5 dozen cookies.

Preheat oven to 375° F.

Oatmeal cookies

1 c. flour
1¼ t. baking powder
½ t. baking soda
½ t. salt
½ c. butter or
    margarine
1 c. brown sugar, packed
1 egg
¾ t. vanilla
1½ c. quick-cooking
    rolled oats

Mix flour, baking powder, soda, and salt. Beat shortening and sugar until creamy. Beat in egg and vanilla; blend in flour mixture. Stir in rolled oats. Chill dough thoroughly.

Shape dough into balls about 1-in. in diameter. Place about 2 in. apart on an ungreased cookie sheet.

Bake at 350° F. for 10 to 15 min. Remove from baking sheet while warm; cool on racks.

Variations. For raisin-oatmeal cookies, add ½ cup raisins with the oats. For coconut- or nut-oatmeal cookies, add ½ cup flaked coconut or ½ cup chopped nuts with the oats. For orange-oatmeal cookies, add 2 tablespoons orange juice and 1 teaspoon grated orange rind to shortening and sugar mixture. Add ½ cup raisins and ½ cup chopped nuts with the oats. Chill dough thoroughly; drop by teaspoonfuls onto baking sheet.

Makes 3 to 4 dozen cookies.

Chocolate sparkles

1 c. softened butter or
    margarine
1¼ c. sugar
2 eggs
2 (1-oz.) squares
    unsweetened
    chocolate, melted
½ t. vanilla
2⅔ c. flour
2 t. cream of tartar
1 t. baking soda
½ t. salt
¼ c. sugar

Beat shortening and 1¼ cups sugar until creamy. Beat in eggs; add melted chocolate and vanilla. Mix flour, cream of tartar, soda, and salt. Stir into chocolate mixture; blend well. Chill the dough.

Shape dough into balls about 1-in. in diameter. Roll balls in ¼ cup sugar and place about 2-in. apart on an ungreased baking sheet.

Bake at 400° F. 8 to 10 min. Remove from baking sheet while warm; cool on racks.

Makes 5 to 6 dozen cookies.

Molasses snaps

¾ c. butter or
  margarine
1 c. brown sugar, packed
2 eggs
¼ c. molasses
2¼ c. flour
2 t. baking soda
½ t. salt
½ t. cloves
1 t. cinnamon
1 t. ginger
½ c. chopped nuts, if
  desired
½ c. raisins, if desired

Preheat oven to 375° F.
Lightly grease baking
  sheet.

Beat shortening and sugar until creamy; beat in eggs and molasses. Mix dry ingredients and stir in raisins and nuts, if used. Stir flour mixture into molasses mixture. Drop dough by teaspoonfuls onto prepared baking sheet; space cookies about 2-in. apart. Bake 10 to 12 min., or until set, but not hard.

Remove from cookie sheet while warm; cool on racks.

Makes 3 to 4 dozen cookies.

Miscellaneous desserts

Miscellaneous desserts

Included in this chapter are some outstanding concoctions that do not fall easily into specific categories.

Fruit desserts like baked apples and sauteed bananas are quick, fresh, and easy to prepare endings to rich and heavy meals. They make the most of nature's seasonal bounty and are usually lower in calories than pastries, cakes, or cookies. For the dieter and non-sweets eater among your family and guests, don't underestimate the glamour and taste of sliced fresh fruit at the peak of perfection. No sweetening or spicing is necessary for these natural desserts. In addition, a platter of whole fresh pears and apples surrounded by roasted nuts and an assortment of dessert cheeses, makes a lovely and effortless dessert.

Custards, souffles and many baked puddings are related since they all use eggs as an integral ingredient. The drama and elegance of a high rising souffle is unsurpassed for a glamorous ending to a special meal. Although timing is important, the custard base can be made hours ahead. Simply beat the egg whites and fold in prior to baking. The adage that, "the souffle will not wait for the guests" is very true. Thus, you may not wish to announce in advance just what the dessert will be. For, if by chance, your souffle falls, you could serve it as a magnificent pudding. A pudding is just that—a souffle-like mixture that rises and falls to a lesser degree. Custards, such as flan, may be baked and most puddings, such as rice and bread pudding, are actually custards. Puddings, such as old-fashioned tapioca or vanilla pudding may also be stirred and cooked on the stove top. Stirred custards are excellent for pie fillings and may sometimes be used as cake fillings as well. Many of these desserts benefit from additions and complements of the dessert sauces presented in the chapter on Candies, confections and dessert sauces.

Another kind of *mousse*, different from the frozen variety is a chilled egg yolk and/or gelatin stabilized mixture that is lightened by the folding in of beaten egg whites. They can be as rich and sinful as the classic chocolate mousse or as light and airy as a fresh fruit bavarian. Most keep well for a day or so in the refrigerator. Gelatin based mousses are also good fillings for pie shells and some cakes.

Apple turnovers

pastry
1½ c. unsifted flour
¾ t. salt
½ c. shortening
3 T. cold water
   (approximately)
2 T. butter or margarine

filling
1½ c. tart apples, pared
   and sliced (2 medium
   apples)
¼ c. sugar
⅛ t. salt
¼ t. cinnamon
⅛ t. nutmeg

Preheat oven to 400° F.

Mix flour and salt thoroughly. Mix in shortening only until mixture is crumbly. A pastry blender, two knives, or a fork may be used for mixing. Add water, a little at a time, mixing lightly. Dough should be just moist enough to cling together when pressed. Shape dough into a ball. Roll out on lightly-floured surface until dough is about 12x12-in. Dot with butter or margarine. Fold pastry so that sides meet in center. Press folded pastry with fingers. Fold ends to center and press with fingers. Wrap in waxed paper and chill.

Divide pastry into six balls. Roll out each ball on a lightly-floured surface to make a 6-in. square. Place about ¼ cup apples on half of each pastry square about ½-in. from edges. When top is folded over, the turnover should be triangular. Mix sugar, salt, cinnamon, and nutmeg.

Sprinkle apples with sugar mixture. Moisten edges of pastry squares. Fold pastry diagonally over apple mixture. Seal edges with a fork. Prick tops of turnovers. Place on a baking sheet. Bake until lightly browned, about 25 to 30 min.

Makes 6 servings.

Apple cheese dessert

6 c. apples, pared and
   sliced (about 6 med.
   apples)
1 T. lemon juice
½ c. sugar
½ c. unsifted flour
½ c. sugar
¼ t. salt
¼ t. cinnamon
¼ c. butter or
   margarine
⅔ c. processed sharp
   cheddar cheese, finely
   shredded (3-oz.)

Place apples in an 8x8x2-in. baking pan; sprinkle with
lemon juice and ½ cup sugar. Mix flour, ½ cup sugar,
salt and cinnamon. Mix in shortening until mixture is
crumbly. Stir in cheese. Spread mixture over apples.
Bake until apples are done and top is lightly browned,
about 45 min.

Makes 6 servings.

Preheat oven to 350° F.

Baked apples

6 large baking apples
6 T. sugar
2 T. butter or margarine
cinnamon (as desired)
½ c. water

Wash and core apples. Pare apples one-third of the way
down or slit skin around the apple about half-way
down. Place apples in a baking dish. Put sugar and
butter in center of each apple. Sprinkle with cinnamon.
Pour water around apples to prevent sticking. Bake
uncovered until tender, 45 min. to 1 hour.

Variation. For cranberry-baked apples, omit the sugar,
shortening, and cinnamon. Combine ¾ cup chopped
raw cranberries, ½ cup sugar, and 3 tablespoons
chopped nuts. Stuff apples with this mixture before
baking.

Makes 6 servings.

Preheat oven to 400° F.

Cinnamon apple puffs

1 c. sugar
1 c. water
1 T. red cinnamon
　candies or ½ t. food
　coloring
1½ lb. tart apples
　(4–5 med.)
1½ c. sifted all-purpose
　flour
½ t. salt
2 t. baking powder
¼ c. shortening
¾ c. milk
2 T. melted butter
2 T. sugar
½ t. cinnamon

Boil sugar, water, and candies 5 min. to make syrup. Pour over peeled and thinly sliced apples in the baking dish. Sift flour, salt, and baking powder. Cut in the shortening until mixture looks like meal. Stir in milk. Drop dough on top of apples as for single servings. Make dent in top of each. Mix together the melted butter, sugar, and cinnamon. Drop this mixture into the dents. Bake 25 to 30 min. Serve warm.

Makes 6 servings.

Preheat oven to 450° F.
Grease an 8x12-in.
　baking dish.

Banana mold

1 pkg. pineapple gelatin
½ c. cream
4 large bananas

Dissolve gelatin in 1 cup hot water. When nearly cold, but before set, gradually stir in cream. Peel bananas; mash with fork, and beat until light and smooth. Stir lightly, but thoroughly, into gelatin and cream. Pour into a glass dish and allow to set.

Note: If mixing is done before gelatin is sufficiently cool, the gelatin and the bananas and cream will separate into layers.

Makes 4 to 6 servings.

Sweet applets

1½ c. flour
2 t. double-acting baking
powder
½ t. salt
½ t. nutmeg
½ c. sugar
⅓ c. shortening
1 egg
⅓ c. milk
1½ c. pared shredded
apples
½ c. melted butter or
margarine
½ c. sugar
1 t. cinnamon

Sift together flour, baking powder, salt, and nutmeg; set aside. In a mixing bowl, add ½ cup sugar gradually to shortening; cream well. Blend in egg, and mix until smooth. Add milk alternately with dry ingredients to sugar and egg mixture. Stir in apples. Fill muffin tins ⅔ full. Bake for 20 to 25 min. until golden-brown. Remove from pan. Cool 10 min. Dip *quickly* in ½ cup melted butter or margarine. Then roll in mixture of ½ cup sugar and 1 teaspoon cinnamon. Serve warm or cold. May be wrapped in foil and reheated at 350° F. for 10 to 15 min.

Makes 4 to 5 servings.

Preheat oven to 400° F.
Grease muffin tins well.

Fried bananas

4–6 ripe bananas
½ c. butter
sugar
½ t. cinnamon
1 T. lemon juice

Slice bananas into bite-sized pieces. Melt butter in skillet and add bananas. Fry a few minutes and sprinkle with sugar mixed with cinnamon. Pour lemon juice on top. Serve with plain cake or ice cream.

Makes 2 to 3 servings.

Banana casserole

6 ripe bananas
½ c. orange sections
⅓ c. sugar, sifted
2 T. orange juice
2 T. lemon juice
pinch of salt

Peel bananas, cut lengthwise, and place in baking dish. Remove membrane from oranges and arrange oranges on top of bananas. Sift sugar over bananas. Add fruit juices to which salt has been added. Bake for 30 to 45 min.

Makes 4 to 6 servings.

Preheat oven to 350° F.
Butter a baking dish.

Cherry crunch

2 cans cherry pie filling
1 box butter pecan
  cake mix
1 stick margarine

Spread pie filling on bottom of prepared baking dish. Pour melted margarine over cake mix. Mix gently until the consistency of cornmeal. Sprinkle the mixture over the pie filling. Bake for 30 to 45 min.

Makes 8 to 10 servings.

Preheat oven to 325° F.
Grease a 2-quart flat
  baking dish.

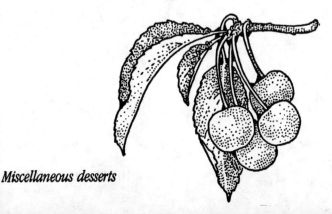

Blueberry-cheese squares

crust
1⅓ c. graham cracker
crumbs
½ c. confectioners'
sugar
½ c. melted butter

Combine graham cracker crumbs, confectioners' sugar, and melted butter. Press on bottom of 9-in. square pan.

filling
2 eggs
½ c. sugar
8 oz. cream cheese
1 t. vanilla

For filling, beat together eggs, ½ cup sugar, cream cheese, and vanilla. Pour into crust. Bake 20 min., cool.

topping
1 can blueberries
(15-oz.)
½ c. sugar
2 T. cornstarch
1 T. lemon juice
or 1 can blueberry pie
filling

For topping, cook juice from berries with sugar and cornstarch over low heat until thick. Blend in berries and the lemon juice. If canned blueberry filling is used, heat, then pour over filling.

Makes 10 to 15 squares.

Preheat oven to 350° F.

Lemon squares

crust
1½ c. graham cracker
  crumbs
½ c. melted butter
⅔ c. brown sugar
¾ c. sifted flour
½ t. baking powder
¼ t. salt

To make the crust, combine dry ingredients; add butter and mix well. Spread most of the mixture in an 8x8-in. pan.

filling
1 can sweetened
  condensed milk
  (15-oz.)
1 T. lemon rind
½ c. lemon juice

For the filling, mix all ingredients well. Spread evenly on top of mixture in pan. Bake for 20 min., cut in squares.

Makes sixteen 2-in. squares.

Preheat oven to 350° F.

Peach melba

1 (10-oz.) pkg. frozen
  raspberries
½ c. currant jelly
1½ t. cornstarch
1 T. cold water
6 canned peach halves
6 scoops vanilla
  ice cream

Place berries in saucepan. Thaw and crush with spoon. Add jelly. Bring to boil; add cornstarch mixed with water and cook, stirring, until clear. Cool. Place a peach half, cut side up, in each dessert dish. Top with scoop of ice cream and pour cooled sauce on top.

Makes 6 servings.

Strawberry bavarian

1 T. unflavored gelatin
½ c. cold water
2 (10-oz.) pkg. frozen
   strawberries, thawed
1 t. lemon juice, fresh,
   frozen, or canned
¼ t. salt
2 c. heavy cream,
   whipped
red food coloring

Soften gelatin in cold water; dissolve over hot water. Put strawberries through sieve or food mill. Measure 2 cups of strawberries; add softened gelatin, lemon juice, and salt. Fold in whipped cream. Add enough red food coloring to tint mixture a delicate pink. Pour into a 1½ quart ring mold. Chill until firm. Invert on serving platter. If desired, serve with canned pineapple slices and strawberries. May also be served in individual dessert dishes.

Makes 8 to 10 servings.

Strawberry shortcake

2¼ c. cake flour
4 t. baking powder
1 t. salt
⅓ c. shortening
¾ c. milk
2 qt. strawberries or 2
   pkg. frozen
   strawberries
⅓ c. water, if fresh
   strawberries are used
¼ c. sugar
1 c. heavy cream,
   whipped

Sift flour 3 times before measuring. Add salt and baking powder and mix thoroughly. Cut in shortening until mixture is the consistency of meal. Add milk gradually. Divide dough into 2 parts. Put on floured board and roll lightly to fit the 2 prepared layer cake pans. Bake for 20 min. or until light brown.

Sweeten strawberries with sugar. Reserve a few for garnish. Crush remaining berries lightly and add water if fresh ones are used. Heat to lukewarm over low flame. Pour half on top of bottom layer; cover with other layer, and put remaining berries on top. Cover with whipped cream and garnish with reserved strawberries.

Makes one 9-inch cake.

Preheat oven to 450° F.
Butter and flour two
   9-in. layer cake pans.

Maple syrup custard

4 eggs, beaten
3 c. milk
¾ c. maple syrup
½ t. vanilla extract
pinch of salt
finely-chopped walnuts

Preheat oven to 350° F.

Combine eggs with milk, maple syrup, vanilla extract, and salt. Pour mixture into custard cups or pots-de-crème cups. Put cups in pan of hot water so the water is at the same level as the custard mixture. Bake for 35 to 45 min., or until a knife inserted in the center of the custard comes out clean. Remove the cups from the hot water, cool, and refrigerate until the custard is chilled. Sprinkle finely-chopped walnuts on top before serving.

Makes 8 servings.

Baked custard

4 eggs, slightly beaten
½ c. sugar
¼ t. salt
3 c. milk, heated until
   very warm
1½ t. vanilla
nutmeg

Preheat oven to 350° F.

Beat together eggs, sugar, and salt until well blended. Gradually stir in warm milk. Blend in vanilla. Pour into six (6-oz.) custard cups or 1½-quart casserole. Sprinkle with nutmeg. Set custard cups or casserole in a baking pan, then put pan in the oven. Pour very hot water into pan to within ½-in. of top of custard.

Bake until knife inserted near center comes out clean, 25 to 30 min. for custard cups, 35 to 40 min. for casserole. Remove immediately from hot water. Serve warm or chilled.

Variation: If desired, 1 tablespoon raisins, fruit preserves, drained fruit cocktail, flaked coconut, or chopped nuts may be placed in each custard cup before adding custard mixture.

Makes 6 servings.

Lemon curd

5 eggs
½ c. butter
1 c. sugar
2 T. grated lemon peel
½ c. lemon juice

Beat eggs at high speed until thick and lemon-colored, about 5 min. In saucepan melt butter over medium heat. Stir in sugar, lemon peel, and juice. Blend in egg mixture, a little at a time. Cook over medium heat, stirring constantly, until mixture thickens and bubbles. Cool, then cover and chill thoroughly, several hours or overnight.

Makes about 2½ cups.

Floating island

1 egg, separated
⅛ t. cream of tartar
2 T. sugar
1¾ c. milk
3 eggs
¼ c. sugar
¼ t. salt
1 T. orange juice
   concentrate (optional)
½ t. vanilla or lemon
   extract

Beat one egg white and cream of tartar at high speed until foamy. Add 2 tablespoons sugar beating constantly until sugar is dissolved and white is glossy and stands in soft peaks. Heat milk over low heat until simmering. Drop about ⅓ cup of meringue mixture onto milk. Simmer, uncovered, until firm, about 5 min. Remove meringues from milk and drain on absorbent paper. Chill while preparing custard. Reserve milk.

   In medium saucepan beat eggs and egg yolk. Stir in ¼ cup sugar and salt. Gradually blend reserved milk into egg mixture. Cook, stirring constantly, over low heat until mixture thickens slightly and coats a metal spoon. Remove from heat. Stir in orange juice and vanilla. Pour into serving dishes. To serve, top custard with meringues. Serve warm or chilled.

Makes 4 servings.

Brazilian pudim moka

3 c. milk
1 c. light cream
5 T. instant coffee
   powder
2 t. grated orange peel
4 eggs plus 1 egg yolk
½ c. sugar
1 t. vanilla
¼ t. salt
nutmeg
1 c. chopped Brazil nuts

Combine milk and cream; scald. Stir in instant coffee and orange peel. Cool 10 min. Beat eggs and egg yolk slightly. Beat in sugar. Add coffee mixture slowly, with vanilla and salt. Strain through fine sieve. Pour into 6 to 8 custard cups, depending on size. Sprinkle with nutmeg.

Place cups in baking pan. Fill pan with cold water to within ¾-in. of the top of cups. Bake for 1 hour or until knife inserted in center comes out clean. Chill. To serve, invert each custard on a dessert plate. Sprinkle with Brazil nuts. Pour chocolate sauce over nuts.

royal chocolate sauce
2 (1-oz.) squares
   unsweetened
   chocolate
6 T. water
½ c. sugar
few grains of salt
3 T. butter or margarine
½ t. vanilla

Combine chocolate and water in saucepan. Stir over low heat until smooth and blended. Add sugar and salt. Stir constantly until sugar is dissolved and mixture slightly thickened. Remove from heat. Stir in butter and vanilla. Stir until blended. Makes about 1 cup.

Makes 6 to 8 servings.

Preheat oven to 325° F.

Russian cream

1 c. light cream
¾ c. sugar
1½ t. unflavored gelatin
2 T. cold water
1 c. sour cream
frozen fruit

Heat cream and sugar in double boiler until lukewarm. Soften gelatin in water; add to warm cream and stir until dissolved. Remove from heat and cool. Fold in sour cream, and beat till smooth and fluffy. Pour into sherbet dishes. Refrigerate 4 hours or longer. Top with fruit.

Makes 4 to 6 servings.

Spanish cream

1 env. unflavored gelatin
½ c. sugar
¼ t. salt
2 c. cold milk
3 eggs, separated
1½ t. vanilla
¼ t. cream of tartar

In medium saucepan combine gelatin, ¼ cup sugar, and salt. Stir in ½ cup cold milk and let stand 1 min. Beat together egg yolks and remaining milk until well blended. Stir milk mixture into gelatin mixture. Cook over low heat, stirring constantly, until gelatin dissolves, 5 to 8 min. Do not boil. Remove from heat and stir in vanilla. Chill 30 to 45 min., stirring occasionally, until mixture mounds slightly when dropped from a spoon.

Beat egg whites and cream of tartar at high speed until foamy. Beat in remaining ¼ cup sugar, 1 tablespoon at a time, until sugar is dissolved and whites are glossy and stand in soft peaks. Gently, but thoroughly, fold gelatin mixture into egg whites. Pour into bowl or mold. Chill until set, at least 5 hours. To serve, unmold onto a serving plate or spoon into individual dessert dishes.

Makes 6 to 8 servings.

Pots-de-crème

6 egg yolks
2 c. half and half or
  light cream
½ c. sugar
6 (1-oz.) squares
  unsweetened
  chocolate
1½ t. vanilla

Beat egg yolks at high speed until thick and lemon-colored, about 5 min. Combine half and half, sugar and chocolate. Cook over low heat, stirring constantly, until chocolate melts and mixture thickens, but does not boil, about 15 min. At low speed, beat chocolate mixture into egg yolks until thoroughly blended. Beat in vanilla. Pour into pot-de-crème cups, wine glasses, demitasse cups or small dessert dishes. Chill thoroughly, at least 8 hours or overnight.

Makes 8 servings.

Mocha pots-de-crème

1½ c. whipping cream
½ c. strong coffee
6-oz. grated sweet
  cooking chocolate
2 T. sugar
6 egg yolks
1 t. vanilla

Combine cream, coffee, chocolate, and sugar. Cook and stir over very low heat until chocolate melts and cream is scalded. Remove from heat. Slightly beat egg yolks. Pour a little of the hot mixture onto the egg yolks. Blend. Stir egg yolk mixture into remaining hot mixture. Add vanilla. Mix well. Strain through a sieve into pots-de-crème or custard cups. Cover. (If custard cups are used, cover with foil.) Set in pan of warm water. Bake for 20 min. Chill.

Preheat oven to 300° F.

Makes 6 servings.

Crème caramel

1 c. sugar
3 eggs
3 egg yolks
2 c. milk, heated until
   very warm
1 t. vanilla

Preheat oven to 350° F.

In saucepan over medium heat, cook ½ cup sugar, stirring constantly, until melted and deep golden-brown. Remove from heat and *immediately* pour 1 tablespoon melted sugar into each of six (6-oz.) custard cups. Blend together eggs, egg yolks, and remaining ½ cup sugar. Gradually stir in milk. Blend in vanilla. Pour into prepared custard cups. Set cups in large baking pan. Put pan in oven, then pour very hot water into pan to within ½-in. of top of custard.

   Bake until knife inserted in center comes out clean, 45 to 50 min. Remove cups immediately from hot water. To serve warm, let stand 5 to 10 min. at room temperature. Gently loosen custard from cups at sides with spatula and invert onto dessert plates. To serve cold, chill and unmold.

Makes 6 servings.

Orange bavarian cream

1 T. unflavored gelatin
¼ c. cold water
¾ c. orange juice
2 T. lemon juice
½ t. grated orange rind
⅓ c. sugar
¼ t. salt
1 c. whipping cream
1 c. fresh orange
   sections, cut in pieces

Soften gelatin in water. Combine fruit juices, orange rind, sugar, and salt; heat to simmering. Dissolve gelatin in hot mixture. Chill until mixture begins to thicken. Whip cream only until stiff. Fold whippped cream and orange sections into gelatin mixture. Pour into a 1-quart mold and chill until firm.

Makes 6 servings.

Butterscotch dream

⅔ c. sugar
¼ c. water
1 unbeaten egg white
1 t. vanilla
1 t. lemon juice
1 c. whipped cream
1 (4-oz.) pkg. instant butterscotch pudding mix
1 c. milk
¾ c. chopped walnuts

Combine sugar, water, egg white, lemon juice, and vanilla. Beat at high speed until mixture forms stiff peaks, about 5 min. Fold in whipped cream. Combine pudding mix and milk; fold into whipped cream mixture. Mix in ½ cup walnuts; turn into flat baking dish. Top with remaining ¼ cup walnuts. Chill several hours or overnight.

Makes 6 to 8 servings.

English toffee squares

6-oz. vanilla wafers
3 eggs, separated
1 c. chopped nuts
1 c. confectioners' sugar
½ c. butter
2 squares unsweetened chocolate
½ t. vanilla

In blender or with rolling pin, crush wafers into fine crumbs. Mix together the wafer crumbs and chopped nuts. Use half the mixture to cover bottom of 9x9-in. pan. Save remainder for top. Cream butter and sugar; add well beaten egg yolks, melted chocolate, and vanilla to creamed mixture. Fold in stiffly beaten egg whites. Pour over crumb mixture and cover with remaining crumb mixture. Let stand overnight in refrigerator. Cut into squares and serve with whipped cream.

Makes 9 to 10 servings.

Orange fluff

3⅓ T. orange-flavored
gelatin
¼ c. hot water
½ c. buttermilk
2 T. orange juice
1 T. lemon juice
1 egg white, stiffly
beaten

Dissolve gelatin in hot water. Add buttermilk and juices. Chill until slightly thickened. Fold egg white into gelatin mixture. Pour into 3 custard cups or a mold. Chill until firm. Remove from mold and serve with custard sauce.

Makes 3 servings.

Lime fluff

1 pkg. lime gelatin
(3-oz.)
1¼ c. boiling water
⅓ scant c. sugar
¼ c. lemon or lime
juice
grated rind of 1 lemon
1 large can evaporated
milk, chilled in
freezer 1 hour
green food coloring
(optional)
1 pkg. chocolate wafers,
crushed (about 8-oz.)

Dissolve gelatin in boiling water. Add sugar, juice, and grated rind. Mix thoroughly and refrigerate until slightly thickened. In a chilled bowl with chilled beaters, whip the evaporated milk until stiff. Fold in gelatin mixture. Add a few drops of green food coloring, if desired. Pour into pan which has been lined with crushed chocolate wafers. Sprinkle top with additional chocolate crumbs and chill several hours or overnight.

Makes 8 to 10 servings.

Butter 10x14-in. pan.

THE DESSERT COOKBOOK

Lemon fluff

4 eggs, separated
½-¾ c. sugar
grated rind of 2 lemons
1 env. unflavored gelatin
½ c. cold water
juice of 2 lemons
1 cup heavy cream,
   whipped

Beat egg yolks with sugar until yellow and fluffy. Add grated lemon rind. In small saucepan, sprinkle gelatin over cold water, then heat over very low flame, no more than 3 min. Cool slightly. Add lemon juice. Add this to egg yolk mixture. Beat egg whites until very stiff. Carefully fold into egg yolk mixture. Fold whipped cream in also. When folding together, mix with a large spoon from the bottom of the pan. Pour into a 2-quart souffle dish and chill until set.

Makes 4 servings.

Chocolate souffle

5 T. sweet butter
3 T. sifted cake flour
6-oz. dark, sweet
   chocolate
1½ c. light cream
1 t. vanilla
4 egg yolks
4 T. granulated sugar
6 egg whites
pinch of salt
granulated sugar
confectioners' sugar

Preheat oven to 350° F.

Melt 3 tablespoons of butter in a saucepan. Remove from heat and stir in flour. Cut chocolate in small pieces. In a separate saucepan, combine with light cream, and stir over a low flame until it dissolves. Pour this mixture slowly onto butter and flour. When smooth, stir over heat until it just comes to a boil. Remove from heat; add vanilla, cool and cover.

Beat egg yolks with granulated sugar until light and fluffy. Add eggs to souffle mix. Beat egg whites with salt until stiff. Fold into souffle.

Grease the sides of an 8-in. souffle dish with remaining butter. Dust with coarse granulated sugar, fill with souffle mix, and sprinkle top with fine granulated sugar. Set in a pan of hot water and bake 30 min. Increase heat to 375° F. for 15 min., or until souffle is firm. Sprinkle with confectioners' sugar and serve at once with a bowl of whipped cream or a pitcher of light cream.

Makes 6 servings.

Cold chocolate souffle

2-oz. unsweetened
   chocolate (2 squares)
1 env. unflavored gelatin,
   softened in 3 T. cold
   water
1 c. milk, heated
½ c. confectioners'
   sugar
¾ c. granulated sugar
1 t. vanilla
¼ t. salt
2 c. whipping cream

Melt chocolate over low heat in small saucepan. Add confectioners' sugar. Gradually add hot milk, stirring constantly, until mixture reaches the boiling point. Remove from heat; stir in softened gelatin, granulated sugar, vanilla, salt, and mix well. Pour into large mixing bowl and refrigerate until slightly thickened (about ½ hour). Whip cream until stiff. Beat chocolate mixture until light and fluffy. Fold in cream and pour into serving dish. Chill, covered, for 4 hours or overnight.

Makes 6 servings.

Cold lemon souffle

6 eggs, separated
½ c. granulated sugar
1½ T. unflavored gelatin
juice of 2 lemons
grated rind of ½ lemon
1 c. heavy cream, stiffly
   whipped

Beat egg yolks with sugar until thick and light in color. Soften gelatin in lemon juice. Dissolve by placing pot over boiling water. When gelatin is dissolved, add it to the egg mixture, with grated lemon rind. Set mixture over a bowl of cracked ice until it begins to thicken. Fold in whipped cream. Beat egg whites until stiff and fold into lemon mixture. Pour into serving bowl and chill for 2 hours, or until set. Decorate top with whipped cream just before serving.

Makes 4 servings.

Cold lemon souffle with raspberry sauce

1 env. gelatin
2 T. water
grated rind of 4 lemons
½ c. lemon juice
¾ c. sugar
1 c. egg whites
1 c. heavy cream,
    whipped

Soften gelatin and water in saucepan; add lemon rind, juice, and sugar. Stir over low heat until dissolved. Chill until slightly thickened. Beat egg whites until they are stiff. Fold into lemon mixture. Add whipped cream. Pour into souffle dish and chill for several hours.

raspberry sauce
1 pkg. frozen
    raspberries (10-oz.)
¼ c. sugar

Partially defrost raspberries. Put in blender, add sugar, and beat 20 seconds at high speed. Strain.

Makes 6 servings.

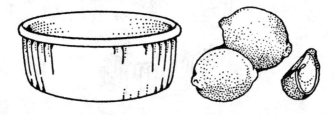

Chilled coffee souffle

2 env. unflavored gelatin
1 c. sugar, divided
¼ t. salt
4 T. instant coffee
    powder
4 eggs, separated
2½ c. milk
1 t. almond extract
2 c. heavy cream

Combine gelatin, ½ cup sugar, salt, and instant coffee in 2½-quart saucepan. Beat egg yolks with milk. Add to gelatin mixture. Stir over low heat until gelatin dissolves and mixture thickens slightly, about 10 to 12 min. Remove from heat; add extract. Chill, stirring occasionally, until mixture mounds slightly when dropped from spoon.

Meanwhile, prepare collar for 1½-quart souffle dish. Bind a double strip of aluminum foil firmly around souffle dish, and extend it 2-in. above top rim of dish. (You may omit the collar and use a 2½-quart dish.)

Beat egg whites until stiff, but not dry. Add remaining ½ cup sugar gradually. Beat until very stiff. Fold in gelatin mixture. Whip cream; fold in. Spoon into souffle dish. Chill until firm. Remove collar, if used. Garnish with daisies made of unblanched salted almonds and semi-sweet chocolate pieces. (Half the recipe may be molded in five-cup mold or turned into 9-in. baked pie shell.)

Makes 12 to 16 servings.

Apple pudding

1 c. sugar
1 c. flour
½ t. baking soda
1 t. nutmeg
¼ t. cloves or 1½ t.
   cinnamon
½ t. salt
4 apples, peeled and cut
   in small cubes
4 T. butter, melted
2 eggs, beaten
½ c. chopped nuts
   (optional)
ice cream or whipped
   cream for garnish

Sift together sugar, flour, baking soda, nutmeg, cloves or cinnamon, and salt. Add apples, melted butter, beaten eggs, and nuts. Stir until blended and turn into greased pan. Bake for 45 min. Serve warm with ice cream or whipped cream.

Makes 6 servings.

Preheat oven to 350° F.
Grease 8x8-in. pan.

Caramel pudding

½ c. sugar
½ c. boiling water
3 T. cornstarch
¼ t. salt
2 c. milk
1½ t. vanilla

Melt ¼ cup sugar in heavy skillet over low heat, stirring until rich medium-brown. Remove from heat. Slowly add ½ cup boiling water. Return to heat and stir until lumps dissolve. Combine remaining ¼ cup sugar, cornstarch, and salt in a saucepan; blend in milk. Stir in caramel syrup. Cook and stir over medium heat until thick. Cook 2 min. more. Add 1½ teaspoons vanilla. Pour into 5 molds rinsed with cold water; chill.

Makes 5 servings.

Indian pudding

½ c. cornmeal
4 c. hot milk
¾ c. light molasses
2 eggs
2 T. butter
¼ c. brown sugar
1 t. salt
1 t. cinnamon
½ t. ginger
1 c. cold milk
ice cream

Slowly stir cornmeal into hot milk in top of double boiler. Cook over boiling water, stirring occasionally, 20 min. Add remaining ingredients, except cold milk and ice cream, to cornmeal; mix well. Turn into baking dish; add cold milk. Bake uncovered 50 min., or until set. Serve hot with ice cream.

Makes 8 servings.

Preheat oven to 325° F.
Grease 12x8x2-in.
    baking dish.

Vanilla pudding

⅓ c. sugar
3 T. cornstarch
¼ t. salt
2½ c. milk
1½ t. vanilla

Mix sugar, cornstarch, and salt; gradually blend in milk. Cook over medium heat, stirring constantly, until mixture thickens. Cook 2 or 3 min. more. Add vanilla. Pour into 5 or 6 sherbets; chill. Or pour into individual molds, rinsed with cold water; chill until firm. Unmold.

Makes 5 to 6 servings.

Bread pudding meringue

4 c. day-old bread cubes
(about 4 slices)
3 c. milk
3 eggs
⅓ c. sugar
1 t. almond or vanilla
extract
½ c. raisins (optional)
meringue

Combine bread cubes and milk. Let stand 15 min. Beat together eggs, sugar, and extract. Pour egg mixture over bread mixture, stirring gently until blended. Stir in raisins, if desired. Pour into 1½-quart casserole. Set casserole in 13x9x2-in. baking pan, place on rack in oven, and fill pan with 1-in. very hot water. Bake until knife inserted 1-in. from edge comes out clean, about 45 min. Remove immediately from hot water and let cool 1 hour.

Spread meringue over the pudding. Start with small amounts at edges and seal to sides of dish. Cover pudding with remaining meringue; spread evenly in attractive swirls. Bake at 300° F. until peaks are lightly browned, about 15 min. Serve hot, warm, or cool.

meringue
2 egg whites
¼ t. cream of tartar
¼ c. sugar
¼ t. vanilla

Beat egg whites and cream of tartar at high speed until foamy. Add sugar, 1 tablespoon at a time, beating constantly until sugar is dissolved and whites are glossy and stand in soft peaks. Beat in vanilla.

Makes 8 servings.

Preheat oven to 325° F.

Easy bread pudding

1 c. dark brown sugar
3 c. stale or dry bread
  cubes
2 eggs
2⅓ c. milk
1 t. vanilla
½ t. cinnamon
¼ t. nutmeg

Sprinkle sugar in the bottom of a buttered baking dish. Add bread cubes. Beat eggs and gradually add milk, vanilla, cinnamon, and nutmeg. Pour over bread cubes. Bake 1 hour, or until custard is set.

Makes 6 servings.

Preheat oven to 350° F.

Raisin-nut bread pudding

2 c. milk
1 T. butter or margarine
¼ c. brown sugar,
  packed
1 t. cinnamon
½ t. nutmeg
½ t. vanilla
2 egg yolks, slightly
  beaten
4 slices bread, cut in
  1-in. cubes
½ c. raisins
½ c. slivered almonds
2 egg whites
¼ t. salt

Heat milk. Stir in shortening, sugar, cinnamon, nutmeg, and vanilla. Stir a little of the milk mixture into egg yolks; then stir yolks into rest of milk mixture. Add bread cubes, raisins, and half the nuts. Beat egg whites until foamy. Add salt and beat until stiff but not dry. Fold egg whites into pudding mixture. Pour into casserole; sprinkle top with rest of nuts. Place casserole in pan of hot water. Bake 1¼ to 1½ hours, or until a knife inserted in the center comes out clean.

Makes 6 servings.

Preheat oven to 325° F.
Grease 1-quart casserole.

THE DESSERT COOKBOOK

Creamy rice pudding

1 qt. milk
¼ t. salt
½ c. white rice
  (not instant)
½ c. raisins
1 c. evaporated milk
2 eggs
½ c. sugar
½ t. vanilla

Mix 1 quart milk, salt, rice, and raisins. Simmer until rice is tender, approximately 45 min., stirring occasionally. Mix evaporated milk, eggs, sugar, and vanilla. Cook 3 min., stirring constantly. Combine mixtures and stir over low heat until thickened. Pour into deep serving dish, sprinkle with cinnamon, and chill.

Makes 8 servings.

Lemon cake pudding

1½ T. butter or
  margarine
½ c. sugar
2 t. grated lemon peel
¼ c. fresh lemon juice
3 eggs, separated
¼ c. sifted flour
¼ c. flaked coconut
1 c. milk
⅛ t. salt
whipped cream

Beat butter and sugar well. Stir in lemon peel and juice. Add egg yolks, one at a time, beating well after each addition. Combine flour and coconut. Add to egg mixture alternately with milk, beginning and ending with flour. Beat egg whites with salt until stiff. Fold whites into other mixture gently, until just combined. Pour into casserole. Place casserole in shallow pan with 1-in. cold water. Bake 45 to 50 min. until top is lightly browned. Serve warm or cold with whipped cream.

Makes 6 servings.

Preheat oven to 325° F.
Lightly grease 1½-quart
  casserole.

Chocolate pudding

¾ c. sugar
1 c. flour
2 t. baking powder
¼ t. salt
2 T. butter
1-oz. unsweetened
   chocolate or 3 T.
   cocoa
½ c. milk
½ t. vanilla
1 c. sugar
4 T. cocoa
1½ c. cold water or
   coffee

Sift together ¾ cup sugar, flour, baking powder, and salt. Melt together in double boiler over hot water butter and unsweetened chocolate or 3 tablespoons cocoa. Add butter mixture to flour mixture. Stir in milk and vanilla. Pour into buttered 9x9-in. baking dish. Mix remaining sugar and cocoa; sprinkle on top. Pour on 1½ cups cold water or coffee. Bake 40 min. Let stand at room temperature and serve cool, but not chilled.

Makes one 9x9-in. pan of pudding.

Preheat oven to 350° F.

Date pudding

1½ c. pitted dates
½ c. milk
1 c. chopped nuts
1 c. sugar
3 eggs
1 c. flour
2 T. butter
1 t. vanilla
1 t. baking powder
¼ t. salt
whipped cream

Mix the butter and sugar; add beaten eggs and milk. Coat dates and nuts with some of the flour. Sift rest of flour with dry ingredients and add to liquid mixture. Add dates, nuts, and vanilla. Bake in shallow pan for 1¾ hours, until set in the center. Cut in squares and serve with whipped cream.

Makes 8 to 10 servings.

Preheat oven to 250° F.
Grease shallow pan.

Fluffy tapioca

3 c. milk
½ c. sugar
¼ c. quick-cooking
  tapioca
¼ t. salt
3 eggs, separated
1 t. vanilla
¼ t. cream of tartar

In medium saucepan stir together milk, sugar, tapioca, and salt. Let stand 5 to 10 min. Beat egg yolks at high speed until thick and lemon-colored, about 5 min. Blend yolks into milk mixture. Cook, stirring constantly, over medium heat until mixture thickens and boils, about 15 min. Remove from heat. Stir in vanilla. Set aside.

Wash and dry beaters. Beat egg whites and cream of tartar at high speed until stiff but not dry, until whites no longer slip when bowl is tilted. Gently fold cooked mixture into whites, leaving small puffs of egg white. Pour into serving dishes. Chill until firm, at least 2 hours.

Makes 6 to 8 servings.

Strawberry mousse

2 c. whole strawberries
2 c. heavy cream
1–1½ c. sugar
2 pkg. unflavored
  gelatin
3 T. cold water

Puree the strawberries in a blender or food mill. Whip the cream with ½ cup sugar until it forms soft peaks. Soften gelatin in water and immediately add to cream, whipping until well blended. Stir in the strawberries and additional sugar to taste. Pour into dessert glasses or dishes and refrigerate 4 to 5 hours.

Makes 8 servings.

Classic coffee mousse

3 env. unflavored gelatin
⅔ c. sugar
2½ T. cornstarch
2 c. milk
8 eggs, well-beaten
4 T. instant coffee
  powder
¾ c. water
2 c. whipping cream

Mix gelatin, sugar, and cornstarch in 2½-quart saucepan. Stir in milk. Stir constantly over medium heat until gelatin dissolves and mixture thickens and comes to a boil. Remove from heat. Gradually stir hot mixture into beaten eggs (a wire whisk works well for this). Return mixture to saucepan. Stir constantly over low heat 2 min. Strain immediately into large bowl. Chill, stirring frequently, until mixture is thoroughly cool. Dissolve instant coffee in water. Stir into gelatin mixture. Chill, stirring frequently, until slightly thickened. Whip cream; fold in. Turn into 2-quart mold; chill until firm. Unmold. Serve with coffee vanilla sauce.

coffee-vanilla sauce
½ c. sugar
1½ T. cornstarch
¼ t. salt
2 c. boiling water
2 t. vanilla
½ c. coffee liqueur

Combine sugar, cornstarch, and salt in saucepan. Mix well. Add boiling water slowly, while stirring. Bring to boil. Boil 5 min. Add vanilla and coffee liqueur. Chill.

Makes 12 servings.

Chocolate mousse

6 (1-oz.) squares
  unsweetened
  chocolate
6 eggs, separated
1 env. gelatin
½ c. cold water
1 t. vanilla
pinch of salt
1½ c. white sugar
1 c. strong, hot coffee
1 pt. whipped cream
  plus 1 t. sugar

Melt chocolate in double boiler. Separate eggs. Beat the yolks until they are lemon-color. Add sugar to the yolks slowly. Add melted chocolate. Dissolve gelatin in water. Pour the gelatin and water mixtures into hot coffee; stir well and strain. Add the gelatin, water, and coffee mixture to the melted chocolate, sugar, and egg yolk mixture. Mix together and add vanilla and salt. (Mixture will be thin.) Beat well. Beat the egg whites until they are stiff and fold them into the chocolate mixture. Beat everything together until the mixture is quite smooth. Oil serving bowl and pour in mixture. Chill overnight in the refrigerator.

If desired, this recipe for mousse may be served with a topping which consists of 1-pint whipped cream plus 1 teaspoon sugar. Spoon on individual servings. Another alternative, especially elegant for a dinner party, is to pass a silver pitcher filled with heavy cream.

Makes 10 to 12 servings.

Chiffon cheesecake

zwieback crumb crust
1¾ c. crushed zwieback
 (about 24 slices or
 6-oz. box)
½ c. butter, softened
⅓ c. sugar
1 t. grated lemon peel

To make the crust, mix together all ingredients thoroughly. Press firmly over bottom of 9-in. springform pan. Bake until lightly browned, about 10 min. Cool completely on wire rack.

filling
2 env. unflavored gelatin
1¼ c. sugar, divided
4 eggs, separated
⅔ c. half and half or
 light cream
⅓ c. lemon juice
3 pkg. cream cheese,
 softened (8-oz. each)
¼ t. salt
¼ t. cream of tartar
1 c. whipping cream,
 whipped

Preheat oven to 400° F.

To make filling, combine gelatin and ½ cup sugar in medium saucepan. Beat together yolks and half and half until blended. Gradually stir yolk mixture into gelatin mixture. Let stand 1 min. Cook over low heat, stirring constantly, until gelatin dissolves completely, about 5 min. Remove from heat and stir in lemon juice. Set aside.

In large mixing bowl, beat together cream cheese and ¼ cup sugar at medium speed until light and fluffy. Gradually beat in gelatin mixture. Chill, stirring occasionally, until mixture mounds slightly when dropped from a spoon, about 20 to 25 min.

In large mixing bowl beat egg whites, salt, and cream of tartar at high speed until foamy. Add remaining ½ cup sugar, 1 tablespoonful at a time, beating constantly until sugar is dissolved and whites are glossy and stand in soft peaks. Fold chilled gelatin mixture and whipped cream into egg whites. Pour into prepared crust. Chill until firm, at least 3 hours.

Makes one 9-in. cake.

Chocolate cheesecake

crust
1 pkg. chocolate wafers
  (8½-oz.)
2 T. sugar
⅓ c. butter or
  margarine, melted
¼ t. nutmeg

Crush chocolate wafers into fine crumbs in blender or with rolling pin. Combine wafer crumbs, 2 tablespoons sugar, melted butter, and nutmeg. Mix until ingredients are well blended, then press evenly over bottom and sides (to ½-in. from top) of a 9-in. springform pan. Refrigerate crust until needed.

filling
3 eggs
1 c. sugar
3 (8-oz.) pkg. cream
  cheese, softened
1 t. vanilla
2 (6-oz.) pkg.
  semi-sweet chocolate
  chips, melted
⅛ t. salt
1 c. sour cream

At high speed, beat eggs with 1 cup sugar, until light. Beat in cream cheese until mixture is smooth. Add vanilla, melted chocolate, salt, and sour cream. Beat until smooth. Turn into crumb crust and bake 1 hour, or until cheesecake is just firm when pan is shaken gently. Cool cheesecake in pan on wire rack. Cover and refrigerate overnight.

topping
1 c. heavy cream
2 T. confectioners' sugar
chocolate shavings for
  garnish

Beat heavy cream with confectioners' sugar, until stiff. Remove sides of springform pan, then decorate cheesecake with whipped cream. Sprinkle chocolate shavings over whipped cream. Cut into small pieces to serve.

Preheat oven to 350° F.

Makes 16 servings.

Perfect cheesecake

crust
- ½ c. blanched almonds, toasted
- 1¼ c. graham cracker crumbs
- ½ t. cinnamon
- ½ c. butter, melted

filling
- 3 eggs
- 1 scant c. sugar
- ¼ t. salt
- 3 c. sour cream
- 2 (8-oz.) pkg. cream cheese
- 2 t. vanilla

Butter an 8-in. springform pan. In a food processor fitted with a steel blade, or a blender with the motor running, drop in almonds. Add graham crackers, cinnamon, and melted butter. Process until smooth. Pat mixture into pan bottom and about 1½-in. up sides, reserving ½ cup for top. Refrigerate.

Rinse food processor or blender and beat eggs, adding sugar, salt, sour cream, cream cheese, which has been broken up, and vanilla. Whirl until smooth. Pour into crust and sprinkle with reserved crumbs. Bake 35 to 40 min. The middle should look shaky but edges should begin to pull away from sides of pan. Do not overbake. Cool in pan on rack for 1 hour, then refrigerate overnight, loosely covered with plastic wrap. When ready to serve, loosen cake with a knife and garnish with fresh fruit, if desired.

Preheat oven to 375° F.   Makes 8 servings.

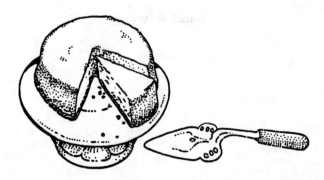

Whipped cream nut roll

6 eggs, separated
¾ c. sugar
2 T. baking powder
1 c. chopped pecans
1 c. heavy cream
1 t. vanilla
1 T. confectioners' sugar

Beat yolks until creamy; add sugar and beat well. Add nuts and baking powder. Beat egg whites until stiff and fold into mixture. Turn into the prepared jelly roll pan. Bake 20 min.; when done cover with wet towel. Refrigerate until cool. Turn out on waxed paper sprinkled with confectioners' sugar. Cut off crusts. Fill with whippped cream mixed with vanilla and sugar, then roll. Ice the roll with whipped cream if desired.

Preheat oven to 375° F.
Line a 11x16-in. jelly roll pan with waxed paper, buttered on both sides.

Makes one 11-in. roll.

Chocolate fondue

12-oz. sweet chocolate
¾ c. cream
2 t. instant coffee

In heavy saucepan, melt chocolate and cream over low heat, stirring until smooth. Remove from heat; stir in instant coffee.

dippers
pieces of cake (pound or angel food)
sliced bananas
pineapple chunks
marshmallows
mandarin orange segments
apple wedges

Makes 6 to 8 servings.

Chocolate cream roll

1 t. instant espresso
  coffee powder
3 T. cold water
6-oz. sweet chocolate
5 egg yolks
¾ c. sugar
1 t. vanilla extract
5 egg whites
pinch of salt
cocoa, preferably Dutch
1½ c. heavy cream
½ t. vanilla extract
sugar

Preheat oven to 350° F.
Butter 11x15-in. jelly roll
  pan and line with
  buttered waxed paper.

Dissolve espresso coffee powder in cold water and place in top of a double boiler with chocolate. Set over hot, not boiling, water and stir until melted. Remove from heat and allow to cool.

Beat egg yolks until thick and pale in color. Add ¾ cup sugar gradually and continue beating until the mixture is very thick and forms a slowly dissolving ribbon when the beater is lifted. Add 1 teaspoon vanilla extract. Add the cooled chocolate mixture. Beat the egg whites with salt until stiff. Fold into the chocolate batter. Pour into prepared jelly roll pan and spread evenly with a rubber spatula.

Bake for 10 min. Reduce oven temperature to 300° F. and bake 5 min. longer until a cake tester inserted in the center comes out clean. Remove from oven. Place a damp dish towel over cake and allow it to sit for 45 min. Remove towel. Dust the surface with a little sifted cocoa. Lay a sheet of waxed paper over surface. Invert. Peel off waxed paper from bottom of cake. Trim edges of cake with sharp knife.

Whip heavy cream until stiff, adding ½ teaspoon vanilla extract and sugar to taste. Spread evenly over cake. Roll up cake lengthwise, using waxed paper to help lift and roll. Transfer to a board or long serving plate, seam side down. If desired, sprinkle with a little more sifted cocoa.

Makes one 11-in. roll.

Sour cream twists

3½ c. flour
1 t. salt
1 c. margarine
1 pkg. dry yeast
   dissolved in ¼ c.
   lukewarm water
1 egg and 2 yolks, well
   beaten
1 t. vanilla
¾ c. sour cream

Sift flour and salt. Cut in margarine. Add remaining ingredients. Mix by hand and chill for 2 hours covered with damp cloth.

Roll out half of recipe on sugared board, fold edges to middle. Roll out again; sprinkle with sugar periodically. When dough begins to be unmanageable, roll to ¼-in. thickness. Cut 1x4-in. strips. Twist and pull into crescent shapes. Repeat with other half of recipe. Bake on ungreased sheets for 10 to 15 min.

Makes about 3 dozen twists.

Preheat oven to 375° F.

Shells to fill with frozen desserts

An attractive way to serve ice cream, sherbet, water ice, mousse, or any other frozen dessert is to scoop it into balls and serve them in edible dessert shells. This makes a dessert more festive and special. How to make some types of shells and suggestions for filling them follow.

Shells can be homemade or bought, and can be filled with whatever filling appeals to you.

Cookie cups

½ c. flour
½ c. sugar
pinch of salt
1 egg plus 1 egg white

Preheat oven to 350° F.

Sift together flour, sugar, and salt. Add the egg and egg white and mix until thoroughly combined.

With a toothpick, make 3 circles on each of two buttered baking sheets. Make the circles by tracing around a small plate or saucer about 5-in. in diameter. Place 1/6 of the batter in the center of each circle. Spread out the batter with a rubber spatula to fill in the circle. Bake, one sheet at a time, until the circles begin to brown lightly around the edges, about 6 or 7 min. Remove the circles from the baking sheet with a spatula. Invert each one over the outer surface of a buttered custard cup. Working quickly but gently, form them into fluted shells by molding them to the outer surface of the custard cups. If more than 3 are baked at a time, the circles will harden before they can be molded. Continue baking and molding the shells. When all have cooled, set them, open side up, on individual serving plates or group them on one large serving plate.

Variations. For Pineapple cookie cups, combine 1½ cups well-drained crushed pineapple with 2 tablespoons sweetened canned coconut cream and ½ teaspoon almond extract or 2 teaspoons maple syrup. Place a scoop of vanilla ice cream in each cookie cup and spoon the pineapple mixture over the top. Decorate with whipped cream and a sprinkling of finely shredded toasted almonds.

For Giant cookie cup, prepare the batter as for cookie cups, and bake one very large circle. Invert it over a large buttered casserole or mixing bowl. Set it on a serving dish and fill with ice cream balls. Top with a fruit sauce, chocolate sauce, or other sauce, and decorate as desired.

For Chocolate cups, make chocolate cups or use bought chocolate cups. Fill them with balls of English toffee ice cream with praline sauce, raspberry cream sherbet, or any frozen dessert.

For Meringue shells, make meringue shells or use bought meringue shells. Put a ball of ice cream in each. Apricot ice cream or rose petal water ice would be nice flavors to use.

For Nutted meringue shells, make nutted meringue shells. Put a ball of chocolate ice cream, frozen orange liqueur mousse, or other flavor frozen dessert in each shell.

For Orange shells, trim a small amount of rind from the bottom of any orange that does not sit squarely on a serving plate. Cut a thick slice from the stem end. Carefully cut out the orange segments, keeping the rind intact. Scrape out the orange cases to remove all the membrane. Notch the edges with scissors. Fill the cases with orange pomegranate sherbet, lemon honey water ice, or bought orange, lemon, or lime sherbet or water ice. Trim with a twist of orange peel, or with some of the segments taken from the oranges.

For Sweet pastry tart shells, make individual shells of sweet tart pastry. Fill with any desired flavor of frozen dessert.

Cream puffs

1 c. water
½ c. butter or
　margarine
¼ t. salt
1 c. unsifted flour
4 eggs

Preheat oven to 425° F.
Grease baking sheet.

Heat water, shortening, and salt in a saucepan to a rolling boil. Stir in flour all at once. Reduce heat and continue stirring vigorously just until mixture leaves sides of pan and makes a ball-like mass. Remove from heat. Cool until just warm. Beat in eggs, one at a time, until mixture is smooth. Drop by tablespoonfuls onto baking sheet about 2-in. apart. Bake 35 to 40 min., or until lightly browned and quite firm to the touch. Outer surfaces must be rigid to prevent collapse on removal from oven. Cool on rack. Slice tops from baked cream puffs and fill with choice of filling. Makes 20 puffs.

Variation. To make eclairs, shape batter into thick strips, 1-in. wide, on baking sheets. Slice tops from baked, cooled eclairs, and fill with a favorite cream pie filling. Replace tops and add chocolate glaze. Refrigerate filled eclairs until served. Makes 10 eclairs.

Variation. To make appetizer puffs, drop batter by teaspoonfuls onto a baking sheet about 1-in. apart. Bake about 25 min. or until done. Slice tops from baked cooled puffs. Fill cooled puffs with meat or fish salad. Replace tops. Refrigerate filled puffs until served. Makes 5 dozen puffs.

chocolate glaze
1-oz. unsweetened
  chocolate
1 T. butter or margarine
2 T. milk
1 T. corn syrup
¼ t. vanilla
1 c. confectioners' sugar

Melt chocolate and butter together over low heat; remove from heat. Add milk, corn syrup, and vanilla. Stir in confectioners' sugar and beat until smooth.

Fillings: Fill cream puffs with any flavor ice cream and put tops back on. Sprinkle with sifted confectioners' sugar or serve with a sauce. Some possible flavor combinations are: pistachio ice cream with chocolate sauce, vanilla ice cream with strawberry sauce, coffee ice cream with English toffee sauce, and mango ice cream with pineapple sauce.

For whipped cream filling, fill puffs with whipped cream which has been sweetened with sugar and flavored with almond or vanilla extract. Replace the tops of the cream puffs and sprinkle with sifted confectioners' sugar.

FREDERICK E. KAHN, M.D. is the general editor for the series of cookbooks to appear under the general title of "Preparing Food the Healthy Way."

Dr. Kahn, a practicing psychiatrist, brings to this series his interest and expertise in the essential nutritional and psychological aspects of personal health. In that vein, he is presently involved in a study of individuals who have suffered from Myocardial Infarction.

He is currently serving as an Assistant Attending Physician at both Columbia College of Physicians and Surgeons, and St. Luke's-Roosevelt Hospital in New York City, and is a member of the Harry Stack Sullivan Society of the William Alanson White Institute for Psychoanalysis.

He is a graduate of the University of Michigan and Wayne State University Medical School.

Index

Index

THE DESSERTS COOKBOOK

— PREPARING FOOD THE HEALTHY WAY SERIES —
ORDER FORM

If you've enjoyed using this book, and would like copies of any other books in this series, indicate the *number of copies of each title* you wish to order, enclose a check or money order for the appropriate amount, and send in the entire page. Allow 6 weeks for delivery.

NUMBER OF COPIES

____ Appetizers
____ Beverages
____ Breads & Cakes
____ Breakfast & Brunch
____ Canning and Preserving
____ Chinese Food
____ Cooking With Kids
____ Dessert
____ Fish
____ Fruit

NUMBER OF COPIES

____ Ground Meat
____ International Meals
____ One-Dish Meals
____ Outdoor Cooking
____ Party Cooking
____ Poultry
____ Sandwiches
____ Sauces
____ Seafood

Please send me the books checked above. I have ordered ____ books at $4.95 each.

	NUMBER OF COPIES	PER COPY		
	X	$4.95	=	$
Plus postage and handling	X	.50	=	$
Total enclosed				$

Mail this form and your check to: Nautilus Communications, Inc., 460 East 79th Street, New York, NY 10021. No COD's, please!

Name _____

Address _____

City _____ State _____ Zip _____

PREPARING FOOD THE HEALTHY WAY SERIES
ORDER FORM

If you've enjoyed using this book, and would like copies of any other books in this series, indicate the *number of copies of each title* you wish to order, enclose a check or money order for the appropriate amount, and send in the entire page. Allow 6 weeks for delivery.

NUMBER OF COPIES

____ Appetizers
____ Beverages
____ Breads & Cakes
____ Breakfast & Brunch
____ Canning and Preserving
____ Chinese Food
____ Cooking With Kids
____ Dessert
____ Fish
____ Fruit

NUMBER OF COPIES

____ Ground Meat
____ International Meals
____ One-Dish Meals
____ Outdoor Cooking
____ Party Cooking
____ Poultry
____ Sandwiches
____ Sauces
____ Seafood

Please send me the books checked above. I have ordered ____ books at $4.95 each.

	NUMBER OF COPIES	PER COPY	
	X	$4.95	= $
Plus postage and handling	X	.50	= $
Total enclosed			$

Mail this form and your check to: Nautilus Communications, Inc., 460 East 79th Street, New York, NY 10021. No COD's, please!

Name _____

Address _____

City _____ State _____ Zip _____

Dear Reader:

We hope that you are enjoying this book, and that you have seen some of the other books in this series. If you would like to order additional titles, an order form is enclosed for your convenience.

Many of the recipes in this book have been provided by outside contributors. We are always looking for additional recipes and would welcome receiving your favorites for inclusion in future cookbooks.

If you would like to send us recipes, please use the form below. **Recipes must be typed.** *If your recipe is used, you will receive a free copy of the book in which it appears. If you need more forms, you may make photocopies of this one.*

Recipe name _____

Ingredients

_____ _____

_____ _____

_____ _____

_____ _____

_____ _____

_____ _____

Baking temperature _____

Directions _____

_____

_____

_____

Serving size _____ *List variations on back.*

Name _____

Address _____

City _____ *State* _____ *Zip* _____

Send your recipes to:
Nautilus Communications, Inc.
460 East 79th Street
New York, NY 10021

Dear Reader:

We hope that you are enjoying this book, and that you have seen some of the other books in this series. If you would like to order additional titles, an order form is enclosed for your convenience.

Many of the recipes in this book have been provided by outside contributors. We are always looking for additional recipes and would welcome receiving your favorites for inclusion in future cookbooks.

If you would like to send us recipes, please use the form below. Recipes must be typed. If your recipe is used, you will receive a free copy of the book in which it appears. If you need more forms, you may make photocopies of this one.

Recipe name _____

Ingredients

_____   _____

_____   _____

_____   _____

_____   _____

_____   _____

_____   _____

_____   _____

Baking temperature _____

Directions _____

_____

_____

_____

Serving size _____ *List variations on back.*

Name _____

Address _____

City _____ *State* _____ *Zip* _____

Send your recipes to:
Nautilus Communications, Inc.,
460 East 79th Street,
New York, NY 10021

NOTES

NOTES

NOTES

NOTES